YORK NOTES

THE HANDMAID'S TALE

MARGARET ATWOOD

Notes by Coral Ann Howells
Revised by Ali Cargill and Emma Page

PEARSON

YORK
PRESS

The right of Coral Ann Howells to be identified as Author of this Work has been asserted by her in accordance with the Copyright, Designs and Patents Act 1988

YORK PRESS
322 Old Brompton Road, London SW5 9JH
PEARSON EDUCATION LIMITED
Edinburgh Gate, Harlow,
Essex CM20 2JE, United Kingdom
Associated companies, branches and representatives throughout the world

First published 1998
New edition 2003
This new and fully revised edition 2016

10 9 8 7 6 5 4 3 2 1

ISBN 978-1-2921-3818-3

Illustration on page 41 by Alan Batley
Typeset by Carnegie Book Production
Printed in Slovakia

Photo credits: Satellite/Shutterstock for page 6 / Viktor Gagarin/Shutterstock for page 7 / © iStock/Juanmonino for page 8 / Joseph Sohm/Shutterstock for page 11 / Andreas Kuehn/Getty for page 12 / photo.ua/Shutterstock for page 13 / © iStock/AlePinna for page 14 / CGIBackgrounds.com/Getty for page 15 / © Guy Moberly/Alamy Stock Photo for page 16 / © Elena Elisseeva/Alamy Stock Photo for page 17 / © iStock/Patrick Banks for page 18 / © iStock/josh-r for page 19 / photo.ua/Shutterstock for page 20 / anneleven/Getty for page 21 / ancroft/Shutterstock for page 22 / GlobalStock/Getty for page 23 / Liljam/Shutterstock for page 24 / tea maeklong/Shutterstock for page 25 / Neirfy/Shutterstock for page 26 / natushm/Shutterstock for page 27 / © Dimitri Otis/Alamy Stock Photo for page 28 / Hong Vo/Shutterstock for page 29 / © iStock/Phillip HofstAtter for page 30 top / Dundanim/Shutterstock for page 30 bottom / Tischenko Irina/Shutterstock for page 31 / MorganStudio/Shutterstock for page 33 / © iStock/Makitalo for page 34 / STUDIO GRAND OUEST/Shutterstock for page 35 / Galushko Sergey/Shutterstock for page 36 / © Buzz Pictures/Alamy Stock Photo for page 37 / vetroff/Shutterstock for page 38 / Elena Itsenko/Shutterstock for page 40 / © iStock/Patrick Banks for page 42 / mihalec/Shutterstock for page 42 / italianestro/Shutterstock for page 43 / © iStock/raddanovic for page 44 / GlobalStock/Getty for page 45 / Andreas Kuehn/Getty for page 46 / PHOTOCREO Michal Bednarek/Shutterstock for page 47 / © iStock/Antagain for page 49 / Jacqueline Veissid/Getty for page 50 / YazolinoGirl/Getty for page 51 / anneleven/Getty for page 53 / PeopleImages/Getty for page 54 / ra2studio/Shutterstock for page 55 / xpixel/Shutterstock for page 56 / © Geoff Smith/Alamy Stock Photo for page 58 / Korn Vitthayanukarun/Shutterstock for page 59 / FotoMaximum/Thinkstock for page 60 / Palmer Kane LLC/Shutterstock for page 62 / val lawless/Shutterstock for page 63 / ARENA Creative/Shutterstock for page 64 / Coprid/Shutterstock for page 66 / Kristian Peetz/Thinkstock for page 67 / Paul Orr/Shutterstock for page 68 / Rumo/Shutterstock for page 70 / © Stephen Orsillo/Alamy Stock Photo for page 71 / © iStock/Juanmonino for page 73 bottom / holbox/Shutterstock for page 75 top / © Ethel Wolvovitz/Alamy Stock Photo for page 75 bottom / © Everett Collection Historical/Alamy Stock Photo for page 76 / Winai Tepsuttinun/Shutterstock for page 77 / © Portrait Essentials/Alamy Stock Photo for page 78 / Marco Secchi/Getty for page 79 / © iStock/BrianAJackson for page 80 / © iStock/siwaphoom for page 81 / Tomazino/Shutterstock for page 82

CONTENTS

PART ONE: INTRODUCING *THE HANDMAID'S TALE*

How to study and revise *The Handmaid's Tale* 5
The Handmaid's Tale: A snapshot 6

PART TWO: STUDYING *THE HANDMAID'S TALE*

Synopsis 8
Dedication and epigraph 10
Section I Night, Chapter 1 11
Section II Shopping, Chapters 2–3 12
Section II Shopping, Chapters 4–6 13
    Extract analysis: Chapter 5, page 33 14
Section III Night, Chapter 7 16
Section IV Waiting Room, Chapters 8–10 17
Section IV Waiting Room, Chapters 11–12 18
Section V Nap, Chapter 13 & Section VI Household, Chapter 14 19
    Extract analysis: Chapter 13, pages 83–4 20
Section VI Household, Chapters 14–17 21
Section VII Night, Chapter 18 & Section VIII Birth Day, Chapters 19–20 22
Section VIII Birth Day, Chapters 21–3 23
Section IX Night, Chapter 24 & Section X Soul Scrolls, Chapter 25 24
    Extract analysis: Chapter 25, pages 161–2 25
Section X Soul Scrolls, Chapters 26–7 27
Section X Soul Scrolls, Chapter 28–9 28
Section XI Night, Chapter 30 & Section XII Jezebel's, Chapters 31–2 29
Section XII Jezebel's, Chapters 33–4 30
Section XII Jezebel's, Chapters 35–7 31
Section XII Jezebel's, Chapters 38–9 32
Section XIII Night, Chapter 40 & Section XIV Salvaging, Chapter 41 33
    Extract analysis: Chapter 41, pages 279–80 34
Section XIV Salvaging, Chapters 42–4 36
Section XIV Salvaging, Chapter 45 & Section XV Night, Chapter 46 37
Historical Notes on *The Handmaid's Tale* 38
Progress check 39

PART THREE: CHARACTERS AND THEMES

Characters 41
    Offred 42
    Moira 45
    Serena Joy 46
    The other Commanders' Wives 48
    The Aunts 48
    Ofglen and Ofwarren 49
    Offred's mother 50
    The Commander 51
    Nick 53
    Luke 54
Themes 55
Progress check 61

PART FOUR: GENRE, STRUCTURE AND LANGUAGE

Genre 62
Structure 64
Language 65
Progress check 72

PART FIVE: CONTEXTS AND INTERPRETATIONS

Historical context...73
Settings...75
Literary context..76
Critical interpretations 79
Progress check 83

PART SIX: PROGRESS BOOSTER

Assessment focus...84
How to write high-quality responses 86
Questions with statements, quotations or viewpoints 88
Comparing *The Handmaid's Tale* with other texts 90
Using critical interpretations and perspectives 92
Annotated sample answers..94
    Mid-level answer 94
    Good-level answer 96
    Very high-level answer..98
Practice task... 100

PART SEVEN: FURTHER STUDY AND ANSWERS

Further reading... 101
Literary terms 102
Revision task answers.. 103
Progress check answers... 105
Mark scheme 112

HOW TO STUDY AND REVISE *THE HANDMAID'S TALE*

These Notes can be used in a range of ways to help you read, study and revise for your exam or assessment.

Become an informed and independent reader

Throughout the Notes, you will find the following key features to aid your study:

- **'Key context'** margin features: these widen your knowledge of the setting, whether historical, social or political. This is highlighted by the AO3 (Assessment Objective 3) symbol to remind you of its connection to aspects you may want to refer to in your exam responses.

- **'Key interpretation'** boxes (a key part of AO5 on AQA – AO5 is not assessed by Edexcel in relation to *The Handmaid's Tale*): do you agree with the perspective or idea that is explained here? Does it help you form your own view of events or characters? Developing your own interpretations is a key element of higher-level achievement in A Level, so make use of this and similar features.

- **'Key connection'** features (linked to AO4): whether or not you refer to such connections in your exam writing, having a wider understanding of how the novel, or aspects of it, links to other texts or ideas can give you new perspectives on the text.

- **'Study focus'** panels: these help to secure your own understanding of key elements of the text. Being able to write in depth on a particular point or explain a specific feature will help your writing sound professional and informed.

- **'Key quotation'** features: these identify the effect of specific language choices – you could use these for revision purposes at a later date.

- **'Progress booster'** features: these offer specific advice about how to tackle a particular aspect of your study, or an idea you might want to consider discussing in your exam responses.

- **'Extract analysis'** sections: these are vital for you to use either during your reading or when you come back to the text afterwards. These sections take a core extract from a chapter and explore it in real depth, explaining its significance and impact, raising questions and offering interpretations.

Stay on track with your study and revision

Your first port of call will always be your teacher, and you should already have a good sense of how well you are doing, but the Notes offer you several ways of measuring your progress.

- **'Revision task'**: throughout the Notes, there are some challenging, but achievable, written tasks for you to do relevant to the section just covered. Suggested answers are supplied in **Part Seven**.

- **'Progress check'**: this feature comes at the end of **Parts Two** to **Five**, and contains a range of short and longer tasks which address key aspects of the Part of the Notes you have just read. Below this is a grid of key skills which you can complete to track your progress, and rate your understanding.

- **'Practice task'** and **'Mark scheme'**: use these features to make a judgement on how well you know the text and how well you can apply the skills you have learnt.

Most importantly, enjoy using these Notes and see your knowledge and skills improve.

The edition used in these Notes is the Vintage Books edition, 1996.

A02 PROGRESS BOOSTER

You can choose to use the Notes as you wish, but as you read the novel it can be useful to read over the **Part Two** summaries and analysis in order to embed key events, ideas and developments in the **narrative**.

A02 PROGRESS BOOSTER

Don't forget to make full use of **Parts Three** to **Five** of the Notes during your reading of the novel. You may have essays to complete on genre, or key themes, or on the impact of specific settings, and can therefore make use of these in-depth sections. Or you may simply want to check out a particular idea or area as you're reading or studying the novel in class.

A01 PROGRESS BOOSTER

Part Six: Progress booster will introduce you to different styles of question and how to tackle them; help you to improve your expression so that it has a suitably academic and professional tone; assist you with planning and use of evidence to support ideas; and, most importantly, show you three sample exam responses at different levels with helpful AO-related annotations and follow-up comments. Dedicating time to working through this Part will be something you won't regret.

THE HANDMAID'S TALE: A SNAPSHOT

A nightmarish vision of the future

The Handmaid's Tale (1985) presents the reader with a bleak futuristic scenario. Margaret Atwood's story takes place in the near future in the new American fundamentalist Republic of Gilead. In Atwood's invented world, democratic institutions have been violently overthrown and replaced by a new totalitarian regime. Due to a falling birth rate, fertile young women like Offred are forced to work for Commanders as surrogate mothers, or Handmaids.

Atwood's novel belongs, like George Orwell's *Nineteen Eighty-Four*, to the genre of anti-utopian (or **dystopian**) fiction. In both novels, privacy, individuality and holding unorthodox beliefs are punishable offences.

A tale of resistance ... and survival?

The story is told in the first person like a diary or letter. Offred provides the reader with a vivid and witty eyewitness account of events, paying great attention to documentary detail. She retains a sense of her own individuality and psychological freedom, refusing to forget her name or her past. We hear Offred's story of resistance in the face of terrible oppression, and of her fight for survival up to the point where she is taken away and possibly rescued from the oppressive regime. Atwood leaves her **protagonist**'s tale incomplete. However, Offred's voice and her story, relayed through the edited transcript of her cassette tapes, remain as testimony to the survival of the human spirit.

A fragmented narrative

On a first reading, we are plunged into a rather fragmented **narrative**, and a nightmarish world where we know very little about what is going on or what is going to happen to Offred. The effect on the reader is likely to be one of shock and bewilderment and then suspense. Only at the end do we get a wider perspective on Offred's fragmented narrative with the 'Historical Notes', though by that point we may have come to believe that the Notes offer a distorted interpretation of the tale we have just finished reading. This disorientation effect is deliberate, for Atwood is challenging her readers to think not only about Offred's situation but also about how the events described in a nightmarish work of science fiction can become an everyday reality.

Gender politics

All the women in the novel are survivors of 'the time before' and their voices represent a range of views about women's role in society. We hear about Offred's mother, a single parent, who identified with the Women's Liberation Movement of the late 1960s and 1970s that demanded equality between the sexes in a range of spheres, including sexual and reproductive freedoms. As she reminisces, Offred comments on her own indifference to her mother's feminist activism and she laments the political apathy of many younger women. Some years later, under the Gilead regime, a woman's function and value in society are biologically determined by her ability or inability to conceive and bear children. The Handmaids' names – Of-fred, Of-glen, etc. – symbolise these women's lack of status or even lack of an identity in their own right.

Political and social comment

In *The Handmaid's Tale*, Atwood challenges the reader to think about the ways in which life in Gilead is both similar and different to our own society. Writing in the mid-1980s, Atwood drew on a range of issues that interested and concerned her at that time, including violence against women, pollution and environmental degradation, human rights abuses, extreme right-wing ideologies and religious fanaticism. Successive generations of readers continue to find sobering parallels between their world and Atwood's dystopian vision.

Reading and interpretation

As an open-ended novel, *The Handmaid's Tale* encourages a variety of possible readings, though this raises the question of how free we are to make our own interpretations. Of course, there is no single interpretation, though there are guidelines suggested by the text and warnings against misreadings. After all, we have a terrifying example of misreading in the novel itself, in Gilead's interpretation of the Old Testament. We would all probably agree that this interpretation is fatally flawed when we see it in practice. Then there is the interpretation of Offred's story offered by Professor Pieixoto in the 'Historical Notes'. His is a scholarly editor's reading of a historical document (transcribed from old cassette tapes) and we may well feel that he leaves out the crucial element of this Handmaid's tale: the personality and private resistance campaign of Offred herself. However, the question on which the novel ends opens up the debate again. Atwood seems to be suggesting that wrong or inadequate interpretations of texts are possible and that we should always actively question the version of events we are given.

Study focus: Key issues to explore

As you study the text and revise for the exam, keep in mind these elements and ideas:

- The novel's **protagonist** and what we learn about her
- The narrative style and structure
- The past, the present and the future
- Women's place in society
- The importance of having a name, a voice and an identity
- Religious fundamentalism
- Violence, control and fear
- Documentary realism
- The **genres** of science fiction and dystopian writing
- Language and power
- The author's purpose

In each case, make sure you develop your own interpretations and, with the help of these Notes, prepare to argue your viewpoint on them.

A03 KEY CONTEXT

Atwood began collecting ideas for her novel in 1981 and kept a clippings file of items from newspapers and magazines that contributed directly to her work in progress. How many of Atwood's concerns in the 1980s remain relevant to readers of *The Handmaid's Tale* in the early twenty-first-century?

SYNOPSIS

Section I Night to Section II Shopping

The novel begins with the narrator's memory of being in an old gymnasium that appears to be like a women's prison. The narrator (Offred) whispers in the dark, in a dormitory patrolled by 'Aunts' and guarded by 'Angels'. The location shifts to a Victorian house, a single room. Offred describes her red costume and her marginal position in the Commander's household. She gets ready to go shopping. Offred remembers arriving at the Commander's house as his Handmaid and meeting his Wife. She recognised the Wife from a gospel choir on TV and knows her as 'Serena Joy'. Offred sees the Commander's driver, Nick, who winks at her, and meets Ofglen, another Handmaid. The two women pass a checkpoint and Offred makes her first small gesture of defiance. Offred and Ofglen go shopping in Gilead and Offred remembers the way these streets used to be before the regime, when she was a free woman. The two Handmaids visit the Wall, from which the hooded dead bodies of dissidents are hung.

Section III Night to Section IV Waiting Room

We learn that Offred has a secret escape route, as she can 'step sideways' (p. 47) into private spaces of memory. Offred remembers Moira, her own mother and her lost child. Ofglen uses the words 'May day' (p. 53) when she and Offred are standing at the Wall together. When Offred returns from shopping, she finds the Commander breaking the rules by peering into her room. Offred discovers a message left by her predecessor – '*Nolite te bastardes carborundorum*' (p. 62) – in her room. While she is thinking back to her college days and memories of her friend Moira, she looks out of the window and sees Nick and the Commander. Offred visits the doctor for her monthly check-up to be assessed for her reproductive fitness. The doctor offers to give her a baby, warning her 'You don't have a lot of time left' (p. 71), but she does not accept his offer. She takes a bath and remembers her small daughter, who was taken from her.

Section V Nap to Section VI Household

We witness how Offred slips away from the present into thinking about her body and her memories. She recalls her failed attempt to escape with her family. The Commander's household assembles for family prayers. In an act of resistance, Offred thinks of her own name, her first contact with Nick, and of her family's failed escape attempt. The Commander enters the sitting room and leads the family prayers. Later, the impregnation ceremony takes place involving the Commander, Offred and Serena Joy. Offred steals a flower from the sitting room and embraces Nick in the dark. Nick tells her that the Commander wants her to visit him tomorrow.

Section VII Night to Section VIII Birth Day

Offred lies alone in bed, tormented by conflicting hopes and fears for her missing husband, Luke. She dreams of her absent family and how times once were. The Handmaids go out in the Birthmobile to attend the birth of Ofwarren's baby. Surrounded by other Handmaids and Wives, Offred remembers her own mother, a determined single mother who took a staunch feminist stance and attended feminist rallies. Ofwarren/Janine gives birth to a baby girl called Angela. It is her Commander's Wife who will rear the baby, as Handmaids are merely surrogates. Back in her room, Offred remembers the story of Moira's heroic escape attempt from the Red Centre. Offred has her first secret meeting with the Commander, where they play a forbidden game of Scrabble.

KEY CONNECTION

In Gilead, Handmaids are fertile young women who have been assigned as surrogates to elite infertile couples. The arrangement has a biblical precedent from Genesis 30:1–3: 'And when Rachel saw that she bare Jacob no children, Rachel envied her sister; and said unto Jacob, Give me children, or else I die. And Jacob's anger was kindled against Rachel: and he said, Am I in God's stead, who hath withheld from thee the fruit of the womb? And she said, Behold my maid Bilhah, go in unto her; and she shall bear upon my knees, that I may also have children by her.'

Section IX Night to Section X Soul Scrolls

Offred is still trapped, but her mood is lighter and she laughs uncontrollably in her room one night. It is summer and Offred walks in Serena Joy's garden. She begins to enjoy her secret meetings with the Commander. She attends another Ceremony and feels more emotionally involved on this occasion. Offred and Ofglen confess to each other their feelings of dissent. Offred discovers an underground resistance movement in Gilead and recalls Gilead's right-wing takeover of America, when women were stripped of their economic, political and legal rights. She asks the Commander the meaning of the Latin inscription in her room and learns who wrote it and how she died.

Section XI Night to Section XII Jezebel's

Offred longs for love and she pours out her desperation in her version of the Lord's Prayer. Serena Joy suggests that Offred sleep with Nick in order to conceive a child without the Commander's knowledge. Offred reflects on her relationships with the Commander and with her predecessor, and feels afraid. In the midst of a mass marriage celebration – a Prayvaganza – Offred sees Janine and learns that her baby died. Ofglen reveals that Offred's secret visits to the Commander are known about. She tries to recruit Offred into the resistance movement as a spy. Serena Joy brings to Offred a photo of her daughter and Offred 'can't bear it, to have been erased like that' (p. 240) from her daughter's life. Offred has a surprise evening out with the Commander. She dresses up, as for a masquerade party. They visit Gilead's sexual underground, 'Jezebel's', and Offred sees its male clientele and the women who work there. Offred meets Moira again, who tells her about her failed escape attempt and how she came to be working in the brothel. In a bedroom at Jezebel's, the Commander arranges a private sexual encounter with Offred.

A01 **PROGRESS BOOSTER**

Consider the extent to which Atwood leaves the stories of each of her characters open-ended, and the unsettling effect on us as readers of not knowing what happens to them.

Section XIII Night to Section XIV Salvaging

Offred has her first sexual encounter with Nick and falls in love with him. Their risky love affair defies Gileadean tyranny, and for the first time Offred wants to stay in Gilead. She tells Nick her real name. At the Salvaging, two Handmaids and one Wife are publicly hanged, while at the Particicution that follows, a man accused of rape is torn to pieces by the mob of outraged Handmaids. Ofglen tells Offred that he was no rapist but a dissenter like themselves. Offred also sees Janine, who seems more disturbed and troubled than ever. Offred's normal life is shattered by the disappearance of Ofglen. She is told that Ofglen has hanged herself. Offred suffers her worst crisis of despair when Serena Joy reveals that she knows about Offred's clandestine evening with the Commander.

Section XV Night

In her room, Offred considers a variety of possible escapes but does nothing, feeling 'pervaded with indifference' (p. 303). She hears the siren of a black van and a team of Eyes led by Nick pushes open her door. Nick whispers that this is Mayday come to her rescue and uses her real name. Offred is taken from the house.

'Historical Notes'

The novel ends with a flash forward to AD 2195 where, at an academic conference, Offred's tale is presented as a historical curiosity. Her fate remains a mystery, and Gilead has long since disappeared.

DEDICATION AND EPIGRAPH

Summary

- Atwood dedicates her book to two people: Mary Webster and Perry Miller.
- The novel has three **epigraphs**, which shed light on the novel's themes.

Analysis

Puritanism

Mary Webster was one of Atwood's Puritan ancestors. She was hanged as a witch in Connecticut in 1683, but survived the hanging and was allowed to go free. Like Offred, she was a woman who successfully flouted state law.

Professor Perry Miller was Atwood's Director of American Studies at Harvard University. He pioneered the academic study of American literature and his two books, *The New England Mind: The Seventeenth Century* (1939) and *The New England Mind: From Colony to Province* (1953), sealed his reputation as an authority on Puritan history. Atwood set her novel not in her native Canada, but in and around Harvard University in Cambridge and Boston, Massachusetts.

Study focus: Approaches to reading **A02**

Atwood's choices of Mary Webster and Perry Miller as dedicatees hint at the Puritan background used for Gilead, and the combination of quotations that preface the novel give valuable insights into approaching the fictional work that follows.

The first quotation, from Genesis 30:1–3, is from the Old Testament story about surrogate mothers on which the novel is based (see Key connection, page 8). It provides the biblical precedent for sexual practices in Gilead, and raises the issue of religious fundamentalism. It also opens the way to a feminist critique of a patriarchal society in which women are regarded as nothing but sexual and domestic commodities.

The second quotation is from Jonathan Swift's essay 'A Modest Proposal' (1729), a desperate plea for improving conditions in Ireland in the 1720s in the form of a ferocious pamphlet that – in a straight-faced but **satirical** way – recommends cannibalism and the treatment of women and children as cattle. In using it, Atwood signals, at the very opening of the book, her thematic and satirical intentions.

The third quotation, taken from a Sufi proverb, suggests that in the natural world, the human instinct for survival can be trusted. It is a comment on the polluted world of Gilead where the balance of nature has been destroyed, and is also an implied criticism of the state's over-regulation of human social and sexual activities.

Taken together, the epigraphs help us to think about the relationship between human nature and the written word, and about the factors that affect human behaviour.

KEY CONTEXT **A03**

The Puritans were English Protestants who believed the Church of England needed to undergo more reform. Many Puritans settled in North America in the early seventeenth century. The word 'puritan' is associated with strict moral codes, plain clothing and furnishings and, above all, a form of worship they considered 'purer', free from Roman Catholic influences. Atwood tells Mary Webster's story in her essay on 'Witches' in *Second Words* (1982).

KEY CONNECTION **A04**

Jonathan Swift (1667–1745) was an Anglo-Irish novelist, essayist and clergyman. The full title of his satirical essay – anonymously written and published in 1729 – is 'A Modest Proposal for Preventing the Children of Poor People From Being a Burthen to Their Parents or Country, and for Making Them Beneficial to the Publick'. He is also well known as the author of *Gulliver's Travels* (1726).

Revision task 1: A puritanical life **A02**

As you read the first few chapters of *The Handmaid's Tale*, make notes on the parallels between Offred's situation and lifestyle, and Puritanism.

SECTION I NIGHT, CHAPTER 1

Summary

- The **narrator** describes a former gymnasium that appears now to be like a women's prison, patrolled by 'Aunt Sara and Aunt Elizabeth' (pp. 13–14) and guarded by 'Angels'.
- The narrator nostalgically recalls the games and the dances that would once have been held in this space.

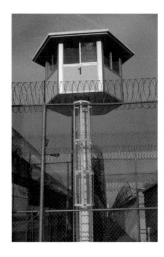

Analysis

Before and after

This dislocated opening emphasises the confusion and fear that characterises any totalitarian state – in this instance, Gilead. The narrator is one of a group of young women who were held in a makeshift prison camp in what was once a college gymnasium, controlled by two women gaolers **ironically** named 'Aunts', with a heavy guard outside. With its references to 'basketball' and 'chewing gum' (p. 13) it sounds very like an American college campus, which indeed it turns out to be. The sheets 'still said U.S.' (p. 13), suggesting that while the location is familiar, 'U.S.' is no longer its name. Specifically, this is, or was, the celebrated American university Harvard, which has undergone a transformation in this **dystopian** novel.

Resisting the regime

This short introductory chapter manages to evoke not only regimental discipline with the lines of army cots and the Aunts on patrol, but also the young women's ability to find ways of resisting the system of control. When the Aunts are not looking, they reach out to touch each other's hands and whisper their names in the dark. Atwood shows us that despite the strict and depersonalising living conditions they suffer, the women described still have the mental freedom to reminisce about the past and yearn for a different future.

In Chapter 1, Offred remarks that in the silent gymnasium, 'the music lingered, a palimpsest of unheard sound' (p. 13) and the image of the '**palimpsest**' is a powerful one suggesting the erasing and rewriting of names, experiences, histories. Make notes about the significance of names, re-naming and un-naming – of people, places, rituals and customs – throughout the novel.

A03   KEY CONTEXT

As well as being used to control cattle, 'electric cattle prods' (p. 14) were used by the police in US civil rights and race riots of the late 1960s. Here the term makes explicit the association between these women and breeding animals.

A03   KEY CONNECTION

The soldiers of Gilead's army are called 'Angels'. They fight in battalions with names like 'Angels of the Apocalypse' and 'Angels of Light' (p. 92) and wear black uniforms. The name is possibly also linked with the New York 'Guardian Angels', a paramilitary force established in 1979 to curb social unrest.

A01

Progress booster: Names and naming

As we begin to read this first-person account, we do not know who the narrator is, where she is, or why she is there. The narrator is not addressed by any name until Chapter 24, when she is referred to by her Gileadean name, 'Offred'. In Gilead, Handmaids are known by the name of the Commander to whom they are assigned. Behind this official name hovers Offred's real name, which remains one of the mysteries in this novel. The chapter ends with a list of first names secretly exchanged – 'Alma. Janine. Dolores. Moira. June.' (p. 14) as they try to establish their individual identities, and of course this raises the question – which one is the narrator's? During the story all but one name is assigned to someone. Could the narrator's name be the missing one, 'June'?

SECTION II SHOPPING, CHAPTERS 2–3

Summary

- The location shifts to a room in a Victorian house that Offred describes in detail.
- Offred describes her red costume, her marginal position and the layout of the house, which belongs to a Commander and his Wife.
- Having been assigned to do the shopping, Offred receives tokens instead of money from the housekeeper and sets out with a shopping basket. She leaves by the back door and goes through the Commander's Wife's 'large and tidy' (p. 22) garden.
- In Chapter 3, Offred remembers arriving at the Commander's house as his Handmaid and meeting his Wife for the first time. She realised who the Wife used to be – a gospel singer called Serena Joy.

Analysis

Life as a Handmaid

Offred describes the daily domestic routines of the Handmaids, and begins to piece together her present situation, building up her account through short scenes and fragments of memory. She describes a room – she refuses to think of it as '*my* room' (p. 18) – where she is virtually kept a prisoner. Her image of the eye that 'has been taken out' (p. 17) suggests blankness, blindness and torture, and references to the removal of glass from the picture and the only partially opening window suggest that there is a high risk of self-harm and suicide.

Offred's actions seem to follow a prescribed pattern, with time 'measured by bells, as once in nunneries' (p. 18). Her old-fashioned red dress and white headgear signal her membership of a group, and an expectation that her body should be covered and her eyes blinkered. She also seems isolated from the Marthas and excluded from kitchen gossip. As readers, we begin to piece together clues and understand that Offred's role seems to be connected with producing babies for the state. Atwood reveals without explicitly stating it that Offred's role in the household is to be a surrogate mother – a Handmaid – bearing a child for the Commander and his ageing Wife. This is clearly not a voluntary agreement but the result of a government order. For Offred it will be a crucial time, for if she does not produce a child she will be sent to the Colonies.

Study focus: The Commander's Wife

The story begins to fill in missing details with the **flashback** in Chapter 3 to Offred's first meeting with the Commander's Wife, when she arrived at the house five weeks earlier to a hostile reception. Atwood draws a clear contrast between the two women, one young and dressed in red, and the other elderly and dressed in pale blue. The rigid colour coding of the women's clothes indicates that in this society their individual identities are lost to prescribed roles, and Offred realises that both women are trapped.

In their tense first meeting, the Commander's Wife asserts her authority and the closeness of her marriage, and the younger woman is constantly reminded of the dangers threatening her if she does not obey the rules, for example the risk of the wife hitting her. Offred's only power in this 'transaction' (p. 25) is related to her ability to bear a child.

KEY CONTEXT

The word 'Martha', meaning a female domestic servant in Gilead, comes from the biblical story of Martha and Mary. (See Luke 10:38–42.) In this society, it will be noted that almost all the characters are designated by their roles, for example, Commander, Wife, Aunt, Handmaid.

KEY CONNECTION

Commenting on Gilead's dress codes, Priscilla Ollier-Morin notes the biblical prescription in Corinthians 11:6: 'But if it be a shame for a woman to be shorn or shaven, let her be covered', and compares it with Aunt Lydia's rule for the Handmaids: 'Hair must be long but covered … Saint Paul said, it's either that or a close shave' (p. 72). See *Lire Margaret Atwood*, p. 38.

SECTION II SHOPPING, CHAPTERS 4–6

Summary

- Chapter 4 switches back to the present. Offred sees Nick, the chauffeur, who is washing the Commander's car. Riskily, he winks at her and she wonders why.
- Offred meets Ofglen, her shopping companion, who is dressed in an identical red costume. They speak to each other using conventional Gileadean greetings and make cautious small-talk.
- The two women pass the checkpoint and Offred makes a small gesture of defiance by teasing the guards, flaunting her forbidden sexuality as she walks away down the road.
- The Handmaids walk to the shops in what was formerly a university town, and is now the capital of Gilead. Offred recognises it all because she lived there with Luke, her former husband, and their young child. In her loneliness she yearns for them and her old friend Moira.
- There are two significant encounters here: one with the pregnant Handmaid Ofwarren (formerly Janine, whom Offred recognises from the Rachel and Leah Centre described in Chapter 1), and the other when Offred and Ofglen meet a group of Japanese tourists. Offred realises that their westernised clothes now look as exotic to her as hers do to them.
- In Chapter 6, the Handmaids pass the old landmarks and pause to stare at the hooded dead bodies of dissidents (doctors executed for once performing abortions) that are hanging from the Wall.

A04 **KEY CONNECTION**

See George Orwell's *Nineteen Eighty-Four* (1949), in which similar abuse of language to that perpetrated in Gilead as a means to hide the truth is a feature of the totalitarian regime.

Analysis

Slaves or dissidents?

Offred, Ofglen and Ofwarren's names **symbolise** their status as slaves to masters whose names they bear, but Nick clearly does not toe the party line, and when he winks at Offred, she senses that here is somebody who is as dissident as herself. By contrast, Ofglen seems totally devoid of personality, but on reflection, Offred decides that this may be out of fear rather than conviction, for the Handmaids are meant to spy on each other.

A repressive atmosphere

Notice how the author powerfully builds up the sinister, repressive atmosphere. The Handmaids' bizarre walk to the shops presents the odd mixture of familiar and unfamiliar which characterises Gileadean society, where ordinary domesticity and military regimentation exist side by side, just as the biblical car brand names (see Key context, right) combine religious fundamentalism with late twentieth-century technology. Gilead's double image of Christianity and institutionalised oppression is confirmed in the visit to the churchyard and the Wall. Looking at the bloodstained head bag on one of the bodies with its 'red smile' (p. 43), Offred determines to try to stay sane under this tyranny by refusing to believe in the distorted versions of reality which Gilead is trying to impose.

A03 **KEY CONTEXT**

The many religious references give biblical authority to the practices in Gilead. 'Whirlwind' (p. 27) comes from Jeremiah 23:19; 'Behemoth' (p. 27) from Job 40:15; 'Eye' (p. 28) from Proverbs 15:3; 'Blessed be the fruit' (p. 29) from Luke 1:42.

EXTRACT ANALYSIS: CHAPTER 5, PAGE 33

This is Offred's account of going out to do the daily shopping with her new partner, another Handmaid named Ofglen. Under the Gileadean regime Handmaids never go out unaccompanied, with the partnership system providing both chaperones and spies. Offred considers this image of two women dressed identically in red, thinking of them as twins both visually and in circumstance: 'Doubled, I walk the street' (p. 33). Outwardly, the Handmaids appear to be the embodiment of feminine submissiveness and companionship. However, as she reflects, this is in appearance only, for the Handmaids are a **parody** of femininity, acting out a masquerade which hides Gilead's oppression of women. These scarlet women are classified as 'sacred vessels' (p. 146) or Sisters 'dipped in blood' (p. 19), representing both Gilead's fascination with and vilification of female sexuality. This hypocrisy about, and state-sponsored exploitation of, women's sexuality is also in evidence later in the novel when the Commander takes Offred to Jezebel's, the secret state brothel, and she discovers women whose existence is officially denied, 'yet here they are' (p. 247).

This first sentence is also a striking introduction to the **motif** of doubles, which recurs throughout the novel. Offred has other doubles as well as Ofglen, such as her predecessor who hanged herself in the cupboard of the room which she now occupies, and there is the Commander's Wife, whose blue cloak is part of Offred's disguise when she goes to Jezebel's with the Commander, and with whom she shares – in a very literal sense – the Commander's sexual attentions. There is also Janine (Ofwarren), a kind of dark double, who represents what Offred might become if she allowed herself to be brainwashed by Gilead. The common thematic element that unites these women is that they are all oppressed by the same patriarchal regime.

Walking along the suburban street, Offred thinks about the houses and gardens she passes, for though they are well kept there is something artificial about this scenario: it is empty, museum-like, for there are no people and certainly no children, in itself a signal of the crisis at the centre of Gilead's social and political life. What Offred remarks on is the parody of family life that is on display in Gilead's public spaces, similar to the private spaces of the Commander's household. At the heart of Gilead there is not peace, but the illusion of it, as Offred had remarked on seeing the Wife in her garden earlier that day: 'From a distance it looks like peace' (p. 22). Atwood shows throughout her novel that this appearance is achieved only as a result of suspicion, fear and brutality. This is epitomised by the way that language is officially used in Gilead, its platitudinous greetings and **euphemisms** such as 'Ceremony' and 'Salvaging' masking darker and more sinister truths.

Offred exposes this false image of domestic security as nothing but dead space 'where nothing moves' (p. 33), and this is amplified in her comments on the difference between centres and borders. Just as the edges of the embattled state are continually shifting, so the limits of Gilead's power are ill-defined. The regime's propaganda encourages the terrifying possibility that Gilead is not just a territorial state but also a state of mind. As Aunt Lydia has told the women at the Red Centre, 'Gilead is within you' (p. 33), which is the ultimate goal in a brainwashing programme in which all the doctrines of the state are internalised by its citizens. This pronouncement is both legitimated and made more horrifying by its blasphemous appropriation of the biblical promise: 'The Kingdom of God is within you' (Luke 17:21).

KEY INTERPRETATION (A05)

For a detailed analysis of how Offred's interior monologue gives us information both public and private about normal life in 'the time before', see Lee Briscoe Thompson, *Scarlet Letters*, pp. 57–8.

As Offred walks along, ostensibly in a pair but really locked into isolation, her survival strategies come into play. She remembers what this locality was like in 'the time before' when this was a professional middle-class neighbourhood, though now all the 'Doctors … lawyers, university professors' (p. 33) have vanished along with their jobs. She does not say who lives in these houses under the new regime (possibly she does not know), but we assume they have been requisitioned by the state and reallocated.

In a characteristic shift in mental perspective via association with place, Offred's memories of this street are superimposed over Gilead's charade of normality, as she escapes into her own private **narrative** of vanished Sunday walks with her lost husband. This technique is also used by Atwood in Chapter 1, when Offred remembers how the gymnasium used to be. She recalls her domestic aspirations to buy a big house and garden in which to live as a family with Luke, and their hopes about raising children, whose absence makes the streets so dead in the present. This is her silent **discourse** of resistance to everything Gilead stands for

and has done to her, just as it is an exposure of the hypocrisy of the regime. More importantly, Offred's inclusion in her narrative of memories from her pre-Gilead past celebrates her ordinary humanity. It also reassures her and the reader that she preserves her secret identity – like her 'shining name' (p. 94) – underneath her imprisoning Handmaid's costume, whose heaviness contrasts with her recollections of 'weightless' (p. 33) freedom in the past.

Study focus: Double vision

Here the important thematic **motif** of the 'double' is introduced: Offred and Ofglen are doubles. Despite suffering from a form of double vision herself, Offred insists on maintaining the distinction between the significance of the colour red when it is blood and when it is the colour of flowers. This clarity of perspective and her continuing belief in the importance of individuals are courageous efforts to avoid confusion, and are typical of her subversive attitude throughout the novel. Her awareness of incongruities is also a way of entertaining herself through language. Make sure that you can comment on how Offred's word associations and thought processes silently and secretly challenge the 'double vision' of Gilead.

Revision task 2: A key motif

Using the motif of the 'double', Atwood explores ideas about what is repressed and what is revealed; what is familiar and what is alien. As you read on, consider the importance of the motif of doubles wherever it recurs in this novel, and make notes about key passages.

A05 KEY INTERPRETATION

See Lynette Hunter, '"That will never do": Public History and Private Memory in *Nineteen Eighty-Four* and *The Handmaid's Tale*' in *Lire Margaret Atwood*, for a discussion of gender difference in the treatment of topics like history, memory and sexuality.

SECTION III NIGHT, CHAPTER 7

Summary

- Offred lies alone on her bed. She has a secret escape route as she can 'step sideways' (p. 47) into private spaces of memory.
- Offred remembers her rebellious college friend Moira.
- Offred's attention then moves to an earlier childhood memory of going to the park with her mother, an early feminist activist, to a burning of pornographic magazines.
- Most painful of all is her memory of her lost child, who was taken away from her by force under the new regime, when Offred was drugged and assigned to the Red Centre to be trained as a Handmaid.
- Finally she comments on her relationship to the story she is telling and her uncertainty about who she is addressing, or whether her story will ever be heard.

Analysis

Private memories

In this chapter, Offred relives memories of the three most influential female figures in her life – her mother, her friend Moira, and her daughter – in three distinctly separate scenes or **flashbacks**. Offred explains that her storytelling is a survival tool. Atwood makes it clear that Offred's private memories are a source of strength, as they help her to maintain an alternative perspective on events. As we have seen, in the 'Night' sections of Offred's **narrative**, Atwood gives her **protagonist** an imaginative outlet from the system of rigid behavioural controls that affect every aspect of her daily life.

Storytelling

Offred says at the end of this chapter that this is an oral narrative – 'Tell rather than write' (p. 49) – which might make us question how this story has survived and taken on a written form, as she has 'nothing to write with' (p. 49) and writing is banned. She explains that even when she is telling the story in her head it is like a letter, a gesture toward communication with others, just as it is her only way to go on believing in a world outside the confines of Gilead. In the context of her loneliness and the loss of her daughter, her insistence that 'You don't tell a story only to yourself. There's always someone else' (p. 49) speaks of a desire to connect and communicate and of a hunger for friendship and love.

Progress booster: Self-conscious narrator

At the end of this chapter, we see Offred as a **self-conscious narrator**, as she draws attention to her storytelling and the reasons why she needs to do it. She says 'If it's a story I'm telling, then I have control over the ending' (p. 49), which suggests she sees her testimony as a construct and believes that there can always be different ways of looking at and recording the same event. The 'doubling' **motif** also recurs here as she **paradoxically** states 'It isn't a story I'm telling' followed by 'It's also a story I'm telling, in my head, as I go along' (p. 49). In these ways – and in the absence of a certain ending – Atwood's novel may be seen as an example of **postmodern** fiction.

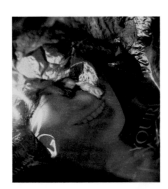

PROGRESS BOOSTER (A02)

There are seven 'Night' sections in total throughout the novel. It always signals 'time out' (p. 47), when Offred's life is not under glaring public scrutiny and when she can thus escape into her private world of memory and desire. What is the importance of this recurring structural device in the novel as a whole?

KEY CONTEXT (A03)

When Moira tells her friend she wrote a recent paper about 'date rape' (p. 47) or acquaintance rape, the narrator remembers her inappropriate reply – a **pun** based on the idea that '*Date Rapé*' sounds like a fancy French dessert. Offred then recalls an earlier memory of participating with her mother in the burning of pornographic magazines, including one which had a 'pretty woman ... swinging, like Tarzan from a vine' (p. 48) on it. By referring to pornography and to sexual attacks against women in this chapter, Atwood is highlighting two key feminist issues in very different ways.

SECTION IV WAITING ROOM, CHAPTERS 8–10

Summary

- On one of their walks together, Ofglen uses the words 'May day' (p. 53) and Offred wonders what its significance might be in Gilead.
- Offred notices evidence of misery and oppression all around her: in the daily executions of dissidents and in a baby's funeral procession.
- On returning to the house she sees Nick, who tries to speak to her. She also sees Serena Joy sitting alone in her garden.
- We learn more about Serena Joy's history and how she became a media celebrity, promoting New Right family values. Offred notes the **irony** that Serena Joy is now a 'speechless' (p. 56) and housebound victim of the very **ideology** she helped to promote.
- When Offred goes upstairs after shopping, she sees her new Commander peering into her room. As she passes him, he tries to look at her face. Both these acts are prohibited, and she is puzzled as to what they might mean.
- Inside the room she now considers to be hers, Offred thinks back to happier times and to her secret, adulterous assignations with Luke before they were married.
- Offred remembers finding a secret message left by her unknown predecessor in the room: '*Nolite te bastardes carborundorum*' (p. 62).
- However, when she tries to find out what happened to the Handmaid before her, nobody in the house will tell her.
- Offred reminisces again about Moira and their college days.

Analysis

Small surprises

Daily life seems to go on as usual; only the weather changes as summer comes in. Yet Offred is alert to minor deviations from conformity, for example in Ofglen's use of 'May day' (Mayday, p. 53) – the standard distress call used by the Allies in the Second World War. Is there a resistance movement here that Offred does not know about?

Here, and in the later incident with the Commander's forbidden glance, Offred tries to work out what these unusual events might mean as one might try to solve a puzzle: 'Maybe it was SOS for ships. I wish I could look it up' (p. 53); 'Something has been shown to me, but what is it?' (p. 59). Atwood's heroine is always alert to details, both to small but significant deviations from the norm like this and even to the seemingly mundane details of daily life such as 'Dishtowels'. These items are 'the same as they always were' (p. 58), and in a world where so much has changed, such 'flashes of normality' are themselves startling to Offred.

Study focus: Waiting rooms

A01

Going to the doctor for a compulsory monthly check-up is the main event in this section (see Chapter 11), but it is useful to consider the other experiences of 'waiting' and of 'rooms' that are described in this section. The events in 'Waiting Room' underline Gilead's objectification of women as passive sexual commodities, though 'room' also hints at the private feminine space which Offred is beginning to claim as her own inside the regime (p. 59).

A03 KEY CONTEXT

In Chapter 10, Offred sings snatches of hymns like 'Amazing Grace' written by John Newton (1728–1807), and old pop songs like Elvis Presley's 1956 hit 'Heartbreak Hotel' (featuring the words 'I feel so lonely, baby') 'in my head' (p. 64), to relieve her boredom. Such songs are outlawed, 'especially the ones that use words like *free*' (p. 64).

A03 KEY CONTEXT

Faith is one of the three primary Christian graces; see 1 Corinthians 13:13: 'And now abideth faith, hope, charity, these three; but the greatest of these is charity.' 'FAITH' is embroidered on a 'hard little cushion' (p. 67) in Offred's room.

SECTION IV WAITING ROOM, CHAPTERS 11–12

Summary

- Offred describes her visit to the doctor for her monthly check-up to assess her reproductive fitness. The doctor offers to give her a baby, but Offred refuses on the grounds that it's too dangerous.
- Offred takes a bath and she remembers her small daughter, who was taken from her.
- Cora brings Offred some food, and Offred waits for the Commander.

Analysis

Offred's body

At her medical check-up in Chapter 11, Offred feels like a dismembered body with only her torso on display and her face hidden. The doctor himself is only partially visible, with just the upper part of his face showing. When the doctor offers to make her pregnant, Offred rejects this offer as being too dangerous because 'The penalty is death' (p. 71). She also fears that the doctor might be a sexual exploiter and that he may be trying to coerce her into a power game in which she would be nothing more than a collaborator and ultimately a victim.

In Chapter 12, Offred is back at the house and prepares for the first sexual encounter with her new Commander by taking a bath. She is overwhelmed by the strangeness of her own naked body and by the sight of a tattoo on her ankle: 'a passport in reverse … supposed to guarantee that I will never be able to fade, finally, into another landscape' (p. 75). This is further evidence of society's treatment of Handmaids like Offred as a 'national resource' (p. 75).

Study focus: Offred's daughter

It's important to remember that Offred has experienced motherhood. The smell of the soap triggers a powerful sense memory of her daughter's bathtime, and Offred longs for her lost daughter. She recalls an incident when a woman tried to steal her daughter in a supermarket 'saying it was her baby, the Lord had given it to her, he'd sent her a sign' (p. 73). With hindsight, Offred can now see that this apparent 'isolated incident' is symptomatic of the worrying changes in society that were unfolding as a consequence of the steep decline in the country's birth rate.

For a few moments, Offred is comforted that her daughter is 'not really a ghost' but a few lines later she concedes that 'She fades, I can't keep her here with me, she's gone now' (p. 73). She remembers her daughter's old baby clothes and the lock of hair she kept as mementoes, and wonders what has happened to these precious things. Overwhelmed by loss, she remembers that her daughter would now be eight years old.

Revision task 3: First-person narrative

What are the effects of the first-person **narrative** on the reader of *The Handmaid's Tale*? Make notes on the various functions of memory in relation to the representation of Offred's character and to the structure of her narrative.

SECTION V NAP, CHAPTER 13 & SECTION VI HOUSEHOLD, CHAPTER 14

Summary

- Offred describes the boredom of her situation, likening herself to 'a prize pig' (p. 79).
- She remembers one compulsory rest period at the Rachel and Leah Centre when her friend Moira was brought in by the Aunts, and relishes the memory of Moira's spirited resistance against the brainwashing sessions in which Janine proved herself the most abject female victim.
- Offred also thinks about male and female bodies. She compares how she used to feel about her own body with how she feels about it now, and describes bodily sensations including her menstrual cycle using powerful and poetic imagery.
- Sinking from meditation into sleep, Offred has two of her recurring nightmares: first her dread that Luke is dead, and then her replay of their failed escape attempt.
- The Commander's household assembles for family prayers. As they wait, Serena Joy switches on the news. Although it is only state **propaganda** we learn that Gilead is a war zone and there are religious and political prisoners and mass deportations.
- In an act of resistance, Offred thinks of her own name and her first contact with Nick.

Analysis

Study focus: The sitting room

The household assembles for family prayers in the sitting room in Chapter 14. The room is presided over by the Wife in her traditional space, though Offred's response to this charade of old-fashioned Puritan values is to see this 'parlour' (p. 89) as a trap like the spider's web in the nursery rhyme. Offred emphasises the room's capitalist underpinnings – 'the sitting room is … one of the shapes money takes when it freezes' (p. 89). She silently casts her eye over the objects in the room and critiques them and their owners' taste: 'a strange blend: hard lust for quality, soft sentimental cravings' (p. 90) – and compares the ageing, childless Wife with the withered flowers in the vase on the table. The Commander's house appears as the embodiment of traditional family values, but beneath this façade lie sexual coercion, enslavement and political expediency. As Offred explains, '*Household*' (p. 91) means a house and its male head: 'The house is what he holds' (p. 91); but there is also her **ironic** reference to the 'hold' of a ship (perhaps a slave ship).

Escapism and a failed escape

Chapter 13 has a very complex construction, characterised by the time shifts between present and past, and between waking and dreaming. The one thing Offred has in her imprisoned condition is a lot of free time, and in this waiting time she escapes her role as passive breeding animal by thinking, imagining and remembering. In Chapter 14, Offred's form of private resistance or escapism is first to consider stealing something from this room, and second to think about her real name. She holds on to that mark of her lost identity as a kind of charm in the hope that one day she will have the chance to use it again in a different future. Using the present tense, she vividly relives her attempts to cross the border and escape with Luke and her daughter.

A05 **KEY INTERPRETATION**

Read Glenn Willmott's essay 'O Say, Can You See: *The Handmaid's Tale* as Novel and Film', where he highlights the double inauthenticity of Gilead in the representation of the Commander's household and in its television propaganda. See *Various Atwoods*, pp. 167–90.

A02

EXTRACT ANALYSIS: CHAPTER 13, PAGES 83–4

Offred's role as Handmaid defines her in biological terms as a breeder, a 'two-legged womb' (p. 146). Yet she manages to survive psychologically and emotionally by resisting Gilead's definition as she writes about her body in her own terms, significantly different from patriarchal prescriptions. In this remarkable passage on the evening of the monthly Ceremony (when her body would seem least of all to be her own), Offred refuses to be subjugated by the Commander's violation and instead she becomes the explorer of her own dark inner space.

Offred insists on chronicling her life from within her own skin, offering her personal history of physical sensations, though the imagery she uses transforms her body into a fantasy landscape. She imagines it first as an unknown continent which she is trying to map, and later as a cosmic wilderness. Her comment that 'only I know the footing' (p. 83) is a powerful description of her knowledge and understanding of her own body, even though it has been seized by Gilead as a 'national resource' (p. 75). To describe the rhythms of her menstrual cycle she uses the image of the night sky studded with stars and traversed by the moon waxing and waning. Accurate in every detail as an **analogy**, this is also a transforming **metaphor**, as the dark womb space expands until it assumes cosmic proportions. Offred's images of immense bodily territories and the later volcanic upheaval of her silent laughter in the cupboard (Chapter 24) have much in common with the ***écriture feminine*** of French feminist Hélène Cixous.

Offred's knowledge and understanding of her own body also extends to knowing the signs of what might be the early stages of pregnancy or the signs that she has not that month conceived: 'these are signs, these are the things I need to know about' (p. 83). Much later in the novel, when she is in a relationship with Nick, she again 'reads' her body's signs in this way: 'I put his hand on my belly. It's happened, I say. I feel it has. A couple of weeks and I'll be certain' (p. 283). But in Offred's analogy in this chapter, when the moon disappears, Offred, not having conceived, is left empty and drained of hope. Her only issue will be blood, whose rhythm she feels beating through her like the sea. This is Offred's own dark female space where time is kept by the body: 'I tell time by the moon. Lunar, not solar' (p. 209). In this way, the passage's imagery also alludes to the connections between the cycle of the moon, the menstrual cycle, and the ebb and flow of the tides.

With her close attention to physical details, Offred not only charts her bodily awareness but also her changing sense of herself under the influence of Gilead's cultural doctrines. She notes that she no longer thinks of her body as a 'solid' object and the agent of her own will, but instead she has learned to think of it as a 'cloud' (p. 84) of flesh surrounding her womb which has become her most important, even defining, physical feature. Atwood's use of metaphor here is rich and suggests both Offred's reluctant acceptance of change in the way she must think about her body and also her continuing need to access a private inner world, both in a bodily and in a psychological sense. Her imaginative word associations and the wide array of images used evoke both a 'fenland' landscape and a galaxy of stars. Although deprived of thinking of her body as 'a means of transportation' (p. 83), the language in this passage is itself transporting and, hence, freeing.

It can then be argued that Offred's position is one of compromised resistance. She is very much affected by her material circumstances as she resents Gilead's control over her, and yet at the same time regrets not becoming pregnant as the system requires of her. Earlier in Chapter 13, she spoke about the treatment of pigs and rats in captivity, wryly concluding 'I wish I had a pig ball' (p. 80) – and in this passage she too is challenging her own captivity and inhuman treatment using all her imaginative resources. She is also all too aware of the fearful consequences if she does not successfully breed: 'I see despair coming towards me like famine' (p. 84). Offred wonders how long she will survive, for 'marking time' (p. 84) reminds her that time is running out and she will be sent to the Colonies if she does not soon produce a child.

SECTION VI HOUSEHOLD, CHAPTERS 14–17

Summary

- The Commander enters the sitting room and there are family prayers. Offred tries to visualise what it must be like to be a man with women at his disposal, reflecting how Gileadean constructions of masculinity relate to power and isolation: 'It must be just fine. It must be hell. It must be very silent' (p. 99).
- The impregnation ceremony takes place involving Offred, the Commander and his Wife. After the Ceremony, Offred steals a flower and embraces Nick in the sitting room in the dark. Nick gives her a secret message from the Commander.

Analysis

Acts of rebellion

At family prayers, the **narrator** builds up the emotional tension, with the Wife's crying being treated 'like a fart in church' (p. 101) and Offred's need to laugh. Offred refuses to pray and instead she silently repeats the secret message written in her closet, linking her unknown predecessor to Moira as a talisman of female resistance to Gilead's sexual tyranny. In Chapter 17, Offred decides to transgress against the arbitrarily imposed rules of the household by stealing something – a withered daffodil – intending to press it and leave it as part of a chain of Handmaids' secret messages.

A01

Study focus: Nick

There is a strong sense of sexual attraction between Offred and Nick, all the more exciting because it is forbidden and dangerous. They embrace unexpectedly and passionately, and it is all Offred can do to drag herself away, although the scene is too strange and threatening to be romantic. Consider the ways in which Atwood juxtaposes and contrasts Offred's encounters with the Commander and with Nick in this section and elsewhere.

The Ceremony

The monthly impregnation ceremony ('The Ceremony') is described by Offred with deliberate detachment where she situates herself outside as 'One' (p. 106) with no hint of the personal 'I'. Offred and Serena Joy are both there on the same bed, as Wives have to be witnesses and participants to this sexual act. Offred and the Wife are holding hands while the Commander has sex with the lower part of Offred's body. As the Wife, with loathing in her voice, summarily dismisses Offred from the room as soon as the Commander has done 'his duty' (p. 105), Offred is prompted to wonder which of the two of them suffers more.

Her detailed physical description and her **ironic** comments on the Commander's performance make it plain that in Gilead the violation of women has been legitimised and ritualised. Yet even here Offred can see the incongruity and surreal human comedy of the situation as 'something hilarious' (p. 106).

A03 **KEY CONNECTION**

The Ceremony is a **parodic** version of Genesis 30:1–3. Rachel and Leah were sisters who became wives of Jacob. Both gave their Handmaids to him, so that he had children by all of these women. See the Bible, Genesis 29:16 and 30:1–3, 9–12.

A03 **KEY CONNECTION**

All the following are biblical references: '*Be fruitful and multiply*' (p. 99) to Genesis 1:28; '*Give me children*' (p. 99) to Genesis 30:1–3; 'Beatitudes' (p. 100) to Matthew 5:3; and 'For the eyes of the Lord' (p. 103) to Proverbs 15:3.

SECTION VII NIGHT, CHAPTER 18 & SECTION VIII: BIRTH DAY, CHAPTERS 19–20

Summary

- Offred remembers lying in bed with Luke before their daughter was born and contrasts this memory with her present solitary state.
- Offred hears the siren of a red Birthmobile and the Handmaids travel together to attend the birth of Ofwarren's (Janine's) baby.
- As she travels, Offred describes some of the reasons why the birth rate has fallen to dangerous levels and why birth abnormalities have become so common.
- Surrounded by other Handmaids and Wives, Offred remembers her own mother. In one of the Red Centre's brainwashing films, Offred recognises her own young mother at an anti-pornography and pro-choice rally in the 1970s. Although their relationship was 'never easy' (p. 132), she misses her and the comparative freedoms they enjoyed at that time.

KEY CONNECTION **A03**

For other ecological warnings by Atwood, read 'Hardball' and 'We Want It All' in *Good Bones* (1992).

Analysis

Building tension

Chapter 18 opens with Offred 'still trembling' (p. 113). In this short 'Night' section, the riot of images combining fear and desire, life and death, indicates Offred's tumultuous private emotional life behind her silent, submissive exterior. Note the intensity of the image of shattering in the first paragraph: 'This is what I feel like: this sound of glass' (p. 113). The author has built up a feeling of tremendous tension.

KEY CONTEXT **A03**

In Chapter 20, Offred describes a 'Birthing Stool, with its double seat, the back one raised like a throne behind the other' (p. 127). Just as at conception, birth will **symbolically** involve both Wife and Handmaid (see Chapter 21). For a detailed analysis of Puritan birthing practices including the Birthing Stool, see Mark Evans's essay 'Versions of History' in *Margaret Atwood: Writing and Subjectivity* (1994).

Study focus: Preparing for a birth **A01**

This section is devoted to the most significant event in the Gileadean domestic calendar, the birth of a child. Gilead dictates that all births should take place at home by natural methods, in the presence of women only. As Offred notes with some scepticism on page 124, Gilead's emphasis on natural childbirth embraces also the idea that the pains of childbirth are women's just punishment for Eve's Original Sin. Offred's account of Ofwarren's baby is a grotesquely comic mixture of birthday party celebration and a description of natural childbirth. However, the celebrations are undermined by female rivalries; the system generates envy and hostility between women – just as Offred also witnessed in Chapter 5 when Ofwarren's pregnancy stirred both excitement and jealousy. Such reactions keep Gilead's women divided and therefore powerless.

Key quotation: Truth and hope **A01**

Offred tries to imagine what might have happened to Luke: is he dead, or alive in prison, or did he actually manage to escape? She says that 'The things I believe can't all be true, though one of them must be. But I believe in all of them, all three versions of Luke, at one and the same time' (p. 116). Kept in total ignorance and tormented by her own painful questions, all Offred can do is hope 'Whatever the truth is,' she says, 'I will be ready for it.'

SECTION VIII BIRTH DAY, CHAPTERS 21–3

Summary

- During Ofwarren's natural home birth, Offred tries to find news of Moira.
- The baby is born and named Angela, but attention immediately moves away from the Handmaid to the Wife who will rear the child. Janine will then be transferred to another family, her reward being that 'she'll never be sent to the Colonies, she'll never be declared Unwoman' (p. 137).
- Offred muses on the differences between what her mother's generation meant by 'a women's culture' (p. 137) and Gilead's interpretation.
- Offred returns to her room after the birth. She remembers the story of Moira's first heroic escape attempt from the Red Centre.
- Offred has her first secret meeting with the Commander, where they play Scrabble.

Analysis

Moira's escape

Returning home exhausted in the late afternoon, Offred tries to raise her spirits by remembering her audacious friend Moira's greatest act of rebellion, when she escaped from the Red Centre by tying up one of the Aunts in the basement and putting on her clothes. As an act of defiance, Moira's escape is both frightening and exciting to the others. Offred describes her friend in dizzying terms: she was 'out there somewhere', she 'had power now', she was 'a loose woman', 'like an elevator with open sides'; 'our fantasy' (p. 143).

A secret meeting

The same evening as the Birth Day, Offred has her first secret meeting with the Commander in his study, and it represents a radical departure from the formality of their prescribed relationship. Aware that it is illegal and dangerous, yet unable to refuse, Offred is surprised to find that when she enters the forbidden room she walks back into what used to be normal life. The Commander's request is a strange one in the circumstances: all he wants is that Offred should play a board game with him, which she does. Alive to the absurdity of this, Offred wants to 'shriek with laughter' (p. 148). She finds herself feeling sorry for the Commander who, she realises, is just as isolated as she is herself. Before she goes, he asks her to kiss him 'As if you meant it' (p. 150).

 A02

Progress booster: The role of storytelling

Notice how Chapter 23 begins with another of Offred's comments on her storytelling and why it is that no story can ever recapture the whole truth of human experience: 'It's impossible to say a thing exactly the way it was' (p. 144). Here Offred also makes a significant comment about different kinds of power, clearly distinguishing between tyranny and control and the power of love and forgiveness. 'Never tell me it amounts to the same thing' she says (p. 145), with the same determination to see and think clearly that she showed in Chapter 6 when she looks at the bodies hanging from the Wall. Make sure you can write about the role of storytelling in uncovering complex truths in the novel.

A04 **KEY CONNECTION**

Read Atwood's 1981 Amnesty International address on the writer's moral responsibilities to bear witness, 'to retain memory and courage in the face of unspeakable suffering' in *Second Words*, pp. 393–7.

SECTION IX NIGHT, CHAPTER 24 & SECTION X SOUL SCROLLS, CHAPTER 25

Summary

- With a newly awakened sense of her individuality, Offred gives some details about herself, her age and her appearance.
- She realises that she may be tempted into friendship with the Commander and remembers a television documentary she saw as a child about a Nazi war criminal's mistress who refused to believe that the man she loved was a monster.
- She sees that she is trapped and says of the Commander's desire for her that 'it could be a passport, it could be my downfall' (p. 154). She finds the situation 'bizarre' and, at the end of Chapter 24, begins to laugh at its absurdity.
- The next chapter opens with 'a scream and a crash' (p. 159), for Offred has fallen asleep in the closet and Cora, the servant bringing her breakfast, thinks that Offred has killed herself.
- High summer comes and Offred enjoys walking in Serena Joy's garden.
- She begins to enjoy her secret meetings with the Commander.

Analysis

In the Commander's study

The secret meetings of Offred and the Commander in his study represent a breaking of taboos and a transgression against Gilead's prescribed pattern of male–female relations. Offred says she would once have taken women's magazines 'lightly' (p. 165) and she says she finds the Commander's needs 'obscure … ridiculous, laughable' (p. 163) and 'banal' (p. 166). All the same, the two of them establish something close to an intimate relationship along very familiar lines, part of the triangle of husband, wife and mistress. When the Commander watches her putting on the hand lotion he has obtained for her, it is all with the hungry pleasure of a voyeur. As the relationship with the Commander develops, Offred realises that the freedoms it brings are small. Despite her pleasure in the word games, she does not forget the unequal power relationship.

Study focus: Garden imagery

A02

High summer has come and Offred walks in the garden, dazzled by its beauty and giddy with desire. Notice how imagery of flowers (both real and synthetic) and gardens recurs throughout the novel: the tulips of Chapter 3, the lily of the valley scent of Serena Joy's perfume in Chapter 14 and the limp daffodils in Chapter 17 are all mentioned more than once. Even the account of Offred's departure from the house in Chapter 46 mentions the 'dusty-rose carpeting of the stairs' (p. 305). How does Atwood use this kind of imagery to draw comparisons between the garden and the house, and what they represent?

EXTRACT ANALYSIS: CHAPTER 25, PAGES 161–2

This passage offers a complex representation of Offred: she pictures herself as a heroine of romance, though through her imaginative celebration of natural beauty and fertility she shows heroic resistance to Gilead's sterile patriarchal power. In the grim circumstances of Gilead, Offred still manages to believe in love and desire and the delights of the flesh. As she says when commenting on her story, 'I've tried to put some of the good things in as well. Flowers, for instance' (p. 279). She is particularly attracted to the Commander's Wife's garden which, though it is enclosed by a brick wall and not available to her to sit in, represents a different space outside.

Offred is fascinated by the garden as an image of the natural world, which celebrates the beauty and fertility already lost in the public world of Gilead and reminds her of her own garden in her past life (Chapter 3). When she talks about the garden, she uses 'we' and 'our' to signal her private sense of possessing its beauty. This is the one spot in the household where she feels a strong sense of belonging. In this lyrical passage, Offred rhapsodises over the summer garden in full bloom, finding in it a moment of release when she transcends her physical constraints and enters into the otherness of the natural world. The flower imagery with its sexual suggestiveness provides an image of her own repressed desires and a space of romantic fantasy, 'a Tennyson garden', 'the return of the word swoon', where traditional images of femininity breathe through the prose as the garden itself 'breathes' (p. 161) in the light and heat of summer.

In this chapter, as elsewhere, Offred explores the overtly sensual and sexual connotations of flowers: 'the bleeding hearts, so female in shape it was a surprise they'd not long since been rooted out' (p. 161) and their importance in the reproductive process: 'the swelling genitalia of the flowers? The fruiting body' (p. 161). Her remarks suggest that the flowers have in themselves a dissenting quality – 'a sense of buried things bursting upwards, wordlessly, into the light' (p. 161) – and she considers their silence to be a sign of their strength and powers of endurance: 'Whatever is silenced will clamour to be heard'. It is for these reasons that she refers to Serena Joy's garden as 'subversive', and hence it becomes a location to which she is drawn and which has an uplifting effect on her.

The garden also puts Offred in mind of poetry, of soft and sibilant words – 'whispers', 'terraces', 'rustles' – and of classical 'goddesses' (p. 161). Her mood is one of new desires and new possibilities. Offred experiences the garden as a place of living colour and movement, a place of delightful temptation, where she hears the willow tree whispering its promises of romantic trysts. In this world of heightened physical sensation she becomes aware of her own body inside her red dress, with the same sensitivity as she feels the grass growing and hears the birds singing. The dynamic natural rhythms are so powerful that she imagines she is actually observing the process of 'metamorphosis' (p. 161) in which things change from one shape into another, so that the rustling leaves and fluttering birds merge together and the tree becomes the bird 'in full plumage' (p. 161).

The word 'metamorphosis' is associated with Ovid's *Metamorphoses*, the early first-century Latin poem about supernatural transformations of human beings into trees or animals. The word 'goddesses' also has classical rather than Christian connotations and suggests images of myth and desire. As Offred watches, everything comes alive, even the brick walls, which become soft and

A04 **KEY CONNECTION**

Alfred Lord Tennyson (1809–92) wrote some of the most sensuous and atmospheric poetry about gardens in the Victorian era. Look at *Maud* (1855): '... the woodbine spices are wafted abroad,/And the musk of the rose is blown ...' and *The Princess*: (1847): 'Now sleeps the crimson petal ...'.

warm like flesh. Of course Offred suspects that her rhapsody is at least in part a sublimation of her own frustrated desires, and she remembers the way in which she teased the young guard who was on duty the day before, wryly admitting the limited props available for her short flirtatious scenario.

This garden is represented as a feminised emblem of sexual desire. Offred's imagination is not attached to the Christian image of the enclosed paradise presided over by the Virgin Mary as the image of female virtue, even though Serena Joy, whose garden it is, wears a blue gardening dress, the Virgin's colour. Instead, for Offred it is a pagan garden presided over by goddesses, and being in the garden evokes a heady combination of feelings filtered through a literary imagination that enacts its own magical transformations. It is a kind of nature mysticism where Offred herself undergoes a 'metamorphosis', changing from Handmaid to ripening fruit like a 'melon on a stem' (p. 162) attached to a natural life-giving source, as she becomes for a moment a part of this pulsating world filled with a yearning for love and the energy of desire.

KEY CONNECTION **A04**

Ovid's *Metamorphoses*, like the *Iliad* and the *Odyssey*, represent the classical heritage of Western literature. The key factor for Offred is that these poems are pagan and pastoral in opposition to Gilead's biblical influences.

This extract shows Offred's characteristic mixture of lyricism and irony, for she knows that this erotic fantasising is an escape from her real circumstances, which are bleak and deathly as winter. However, her impressive energy defies Gilead's master **narrative** of phallic power underpinned by the Bible.

Revision task 4: Laughter **A02**

On page 156, Offred hears something 'inside my body … Noise' and knows that 'If I let the noise get out into the air it will be laughter, too loud, too much of it'. Make notes on how you might interpret Offred's outburst of laughter and attempts to stifle it at the end of Chapter 24. Look for other examples in the novel of Offred's need to laugh, and assess their meaning and significance.

SECTION X SOUL SCROLLS, CHAPTERS 26–7

Summary

- Offred attends another Ceremony. The Commander tries to touch her face but Offred is afraid of the consequences, warning him that he could get her 'transferred … To the Colonies … Or worse' (p. 171).
- Offred and Ofglen go shopping together. After visiting the Wall, they visit 'the store known as Soul Scrolls' (p. 175), where there are computers that print and read out prayers as a sign of customers' piety.
- Offred and Ofglen confess to each other their feelings of dissent, and Offred discovers an underground resistance in Gilead.
- Outside, there is a commotion as 'Two Eyes, in grey suits' (p. 178) grab a man from the street, slam him against the side of their black van, violently immobilise him and take him away.

Analysis

State power

Offred becomes aware of the dangers of her friendship with the Commander when the time comes around for the monthly Ceremony. She is now emotionally involved, and this inevitably complicates her relationship both with him and his Wife, for she now also takes the role of his mistress, not merely that of his Handmaid. Offred is aware that state control cannot function if people see each other as individuals. However, the chapter ends with a sharp reminder of the power of the regime as a man is brutally beaten up by the secret police in the street and nobody dares to take any notice. Offred realises the limits of her courage when she admits to herself that she is glad she is not the victim.

Study focus: Piety and dissent **A01**

Another new perspective opens up for Offred in Chapter 27. Her private thoughts about the 'Soul Scrolls' store are typically subversive: she uses the disrespectful term 'Holy Rollers' (p. 175) to describe the printing machines, tries to recall what used to be sold from the store – 'I think it was lingerie' (p. 176) – and implies that the reasons people print out prayers have more to do with the appearance of piety rather than an expression of actual faith: 'so of course the Commanders' Wives do it a lot. It helps their husbands' careers' (p. 176).

Subversive ideas are also spoken out loud in this chapter by both Ofglen and Offred. Ofglen asks a surprising question which amounts to treason in Gilead: 'Do you think God listens … to these machines?' to which Offred answers 'No' (p. 177). In this way, both women have fundamentally challenged the beliefs on which Gileadean **ideology** is based. Ofglen's revelation that she is a member of an underground resistance group gives Offred a surge of new hope 'rising in me, like sap in a tree' (p. 178).

A03 KEY CONTEXT

Like so much else in Gilead, the stores 'Daily Bread' and 'Loaves and Fishes' (p. 173) take their names from the Bible. 'Daily bread' features in the Lord's Prayer while 'loaves and fishes' is a reference to Christ's miracle of the loaves and fishes, see Mark 6:38–44. 'Tibetan prayer wheels' (p. 177) are cylindrical boxes inscribed with prayers, revolving on a spindle, used especially by the Buddhists of Tibet.

Revision task 5: Violence **A01**

Using the last part of Chapter 27 as your starting point, make notes on the ways in which violence is presented in the novel.

SECTION X SOUL SCROLLS, CHAPTERS 28–9

Summary

- Offred thinks about her relationship with the Commander. Trying to see it as Moira might have done, she realises that there are parallels with her early relationship with Luke, for that too was a form of love triangle: she was his mistress before she was his wife.
- Offred recalls Gilead's right-wing takeover of American congressional government, when women were stripped of their economic, political and legal rights.
- During one of their meetings, Offred asks the Commander the meaning of the Latin inscription in her room. At the end of Chapter 29, Offred finds out that her predecessor committed suicide.

Analysis

Memories of the coup

In Chapter 28, Offred recalls how the Gileadean regime came to power by a violent coup d'état 'when they shot the President and machine-gunned the Congress and the army declared a state of emergency' (pp. 182–3). Offred then describes how the regime proceeded to implement its policies by stripping citizens of their political and legal rights. Atwood's account of the mechanics for a fundamentalist takeover of society speculates on the links between religious fanaticism, militarism and computerised technology. Gilead's social policies were specifically directed against women, and married women were forcibly removed from the labour market and their bank accounts transferred to their husbands. Women were returned to the home in Gilead's effort to bolster the family structure for the moral good of society.

What Offred remembers most clearly is her own state of shock, resentment at the loss of her economic freedom and anger against Luke for still having a job when hers had been taken away from her. She realises how all the advances by feminism in the 1970s and 1980s, for which her mother had crusaded, could be swept away by simply changing computer databases. Offred's memories told in **flashback** also convey a sense of the growing threat of violence, from the menacing presence of uniformed men with machine guns in the corridor of Offred's workplace on page 186 to the violent response to protest marches described on page 189.

'Nolite te bastardes carborundorum'

In a switch back to the present, Offred sees Nick's signal that she is to meet the Commander again and wonders what Nick thinks of the arrangement. In the Commander's study, Offred now feels at ease playing Scrabble and reading voraciously, and on this visit she dares to ask him the meaning of the message in her closet. When he explains that it is a schoolboy-type Latin joke and shows her where he has it written down in his study, Offred realises that her predecessor must have learnt it from the Commander too and that probably her predecessor's relationship with him had been similar to her own. When he asks Offred if she would like something as a kind of payment for her time spent with him, she reveals her desire for some factual knowledge beyond the censored newscasts when she says that above all she would like to know 'What's going on' (p. 198) in Gilead.

KEY CONNECTION

As she holds the Commander's pen and writes, Offred recalls that one of the Red Centre mottoes was 'Pen Is Envy' (p. 196), a corruption of Freudian psychoanalytic theory which presents 'penis envy' as a stage of female psychosexual development.

KEY CONNECTION

The Old Testament story in 'The Book of Job' (p. 182) is, like Offred's tale, a series of catastrophes recounted by the survivors.

SECTION XI NIGHT, CHAPTER 30 & SECTION XII JEZEBEL'S, CHAPTERS 31–2

SUMMARY

- Offred sees Nick and remembers their earlier encounter. She realises that Luke and her daughter are beginning to seem like fading 'ghosts at daybreak' (p. 203).
- Serena Joy suggests that Offred secretly sleep with Nick in order to conceive a child.
- To seal the bargain, Serena gives Offred an illegal cigarette, and tells her where to find a match, and offers to let her see a photograph of her daughter. Offred is angry that Serena Joy has kept her daughter's fate secret from her for so long.
- Offred thinks about her predecessor and about what she could do with the match.

Analysis

Offred's prayer

At the end of Chapter 30, Offred says the Lord's Prayer – her own **ironic** version spoken in anguish, deliberately confusing the literal and **symbolic** meanings of the words. Though she tries to cling to the key Christian concepts of forgiveness and hope in the fallen world of Gilead, she is tempted to commit suicide like her predecessor. Finally she gives way to a cry of despair at her own isolation and imprisonment and her fading hopes of release. She craves communication – 'I wish You'd answer. I feel so alone' (p. 205) – and momentarily she doubts her ability to survive.

Secret alliances

Outwardly life goes on much as usual for Offred as she moves discreetly between her room and her shopping expeditions with Ofglen. Yet beneath the rules there are signs of women's resistance – not only Ofglen's secret network, but also Serena Joy's surprising offer and their secret pact. Offred knows she is being used, but she also recognises that both Wife and Handmaid have become conspirators working in secret together to subvert Gilead's rules.

Study focus: Increasing tension **A02**

Notice how Atwood creates an atmosphere of increasing tension, symbolised by the stifling heat. When Offred lies down on her bed at the end of Chapter 32, she stares up at the blank space where the light fitting used to be: it was from that fitting that her predecessor hanged herself. Identifying with her, Offred has a strong sense of being suffocated or already dead: 'Sometimes I think she's still in here, with me. I feel buried' (p. 223). By contrast, however, these chapters also feature a number of hopeful examples of Gilead's customs and **ideology** being subverted with the quiet strength of 'night-blooming flowers' (p. 201), and of events coming to a head, in much the same way as Offred hopes for a 'thunderstorm' (p. 222) to make the air 'clear … and lighter'.

Revision task 6: Despair and hope **A02**

As you read Offred's story, make notes on how Atwood manages to strike a balance between despair and hope.

A03 KEY CONTEXT

Compare Offred's comment 'Context is all; or is it ripeness?' (p. 202) with the line that appears in Shakespeare's *King Lear*, Act 5 Scene 2: 'Ripeness is all'. The phrase 'Context is all' also features in Chapter 24 (p. 154).

A03 KEY CONTEXT

The phrase 'I tell time by the moon. Lunar, not solar' (p. 209) underscores the fact that Offred's life is regulated by her menstrual cycle – once thought to be connected with the cycle of the moon.

KEY CONTEXT A03

Atwood refers to popular rhyming games that mention common flowers on page 224. In *'Do you like butter?'* buttercups were held under the chin to see their yellow reflection. In *'Blow, and you tell the time'* you puffed at dandelions gone to seed. In 'daisies for love' you pulled off the petals and counted them to the words 'He loves me, he loves me not'.

KEY CONTEXT A03

Offred remembers with pleasure Moira's comment 'There is a Bomb in Gilead' (p. 230), her irreverent **pun** on an American folk hymn, the opening words of which are: 'There is a balm in Gilead to make the wounded whole/There is a balm in Gilead to heal the sin-sick soul'. (A balm heals or gives comfort.) It is based on the Old Testament prophet Jeremiah's question, 'Is there no balm in Gilead; is there no physician there?' (Jeremiah 8:22). Offred delights in the exposure of Gilead's fraudulent biblical **rhetoric**.

SECTION XII JEZEBEL'S, CHAPTERS 33–4

SUMMARY

- Offred is taken on another of the Handmaids' compulsory outings, this time to a women's Prayvaganza to celebrate a mass wedding. Offred describes it as being like a circus or a theatrical performance.

- At the Prayvaganza, in the midst of the mass marriage celebration, Offred sees Janine, whose baby was deemed 'a shredder' (p. 226) and destroyed.

- Offred remembers Janine almost having a nervous breakdown at the Red Centre, from which Moira saved her before trying to escape.

- Offred remembers her Commander explaining to her why he condones 'Arranged marriages' rather than *'falling in love'* (p. 232).

- Ofglen reveals that Offred's secret visits to the Commander are known about and tries to recruit Offred into the resistance movement as a spy.

Analysis

Gileadean ideology

The Prayvaganza in Chapters 33 and 34 focuses on Gilead's New Right **ideology** as spelt out to Offred by the Commander, according to which traditional male domination over women is justified as God's law. The arranged mass marriages between soldiers and daughters of Gileadean officials provide the occasion for laying down the law on woman's subjection and silence, endorsed here by quotations from Timothy (1 Timothy 2:9–15). In Gilead, a woman is defined by her biological destiny, and romantic love is dismissed as a brief ripple in the history of the human race. But the irreverent comments by Offred and Ofglen suggest a general scepticism towards this doctrine. Atwood again shows us that, in an authoritarian society, subversive humour is essential for those who wish to remain sane.

Study focus: A casualty of the system A01

Notice how, throughout the text, Atwood presents Janine as a casualty of the system. Offred thinks that it is typical of Janine 'to decide the baby's flaws were due to her alone' and adds that 'people will do anything rather than admit that their lives have no meaning. No use … No plot' (p. 227). Both in the **flashback** to the Red Centre and at the Prayvaganza, Janine appears a fragile and lonely figure with her 'white and peaked' (p. 226) face and 'thin bowed shoulders' (p. 227).

Revision task 7: Janine A01

What do we learn about Janine's experiences of suffering and exploitation under the Gileadean regime and before? Make notes on how Atwood writes about her and about how she is treated by others throughout the novel.

SECTION XII JEZEBEL'S, CHAPTERS 35–7

Summary

- Offred is alone in her room once again. She remembers her family's failed escape attempt and is filled with nostalgia for the outmoded habit of falling in love.
- Serena Joy brings to Offred the photograph of Offred's daughter she promised to show her. After a minute Serena Joy has to take the photo away again. Offred feels 'obliterated' (p. 240) from her daughter's life.
- Offred has a surprise evening out with the Commander. Nick drives them on this clandestine outing, but Offred cannot tell whether he approves or disapproves of what she is doing.
- They finally arrive at the masquerade party at a place known as 'Jezebel's'. The location used to be a hotel where Offred came with Luke during their affair. It is now Jezebel's state brothel, Gilead's sexual underground.
- Offred observes Jezebel's male clientèle and the women who work there, whom she describes as 'tropical, they are dressed in all kinds of bright festive gear' (p. 246). She suddenly sees Moira and, by their old secret signal, they agree to meet in the women's washroom.

Analysis

Dressing up

The Commander breaks all the rules by inviting Offred to dress up and go out with him one evening. It is a bizarre enterprise as well as a dangerous one, but Offred accepts, partly because she cannot refuse and partly because she craves some excitement. The Commander produces an old purple satin costume with feathers and sequins, plus high-heeled shoes, and he even supplies make-up, a mirror and a blue cloak borrowed secretly from his Wife. This is an **irony** not lost on Offred, who sees herself now as Serena's **double**. Her wry self-description makes it plain that her costume is a **parody** of feminine glamour.

Jezebel's

Forbidden under Gilead's puritanical rules, Jezebel's is nevertheless run by the state as a brothel for officers and foreign trade delegations. The women dress up in Bunny Girl costumes, as devils and as *femmes fatales*, playing out male fantasies about women. These women are here because they refused to be assimilated as Handmaids, and their only alternative to being sent to the Colonies was to join the staff at the brothel. They are not classed as 'people' but as sexual objects for rent and 'officially' they do not exist. There is a **paradox** here: it may appear that the Commander is taking Offred out to give her a feeling of freedom, but he takes her to a place where women are at their most debased.

Key quotation: 'No white wings' **A02**

Ironically, although dressed at the outset as a Wife, Offred is soon asked to play the role of 'an evening rental' (p. 245) or prostitute. However her costume gives her a very literal sense of freedom in that she can for once see freely: 'I can stare, here … there are no white wings to keep me from it' (p. 246). Consider the relationship between clothing, identity and status in these chapters and in the novel as a whole.

A01 PROGRESS BOOSTER

Analyse the **narrative** significance of the variety of forms and media that are used and written about in this novel: photographs, cassette recordings, news bulletins, the films shown at the Red Centre, prayers, a transcript of conference proceedings, etc.

A03 KEY CONTEXT

Jezebel was a Phoenician princess and wife of King Ahab, king of northern Israel. Her story, in which she incites her husband to follow her gods rather than Yahweh, and is severely punished, is told in the Bible in Kings 1:16–21 and Kings 2:9. The word 'Jezebel' has come to be synonymous with an immoral and deceitful woman, and also has connotations of a woman who ostentatiously adorns herself with make-up, wigs and other finery. By choosing this name, Atwood alerts us further to the hypocrisy and sexism that characterise the military dictatorship of Gilead.

SECTION XII JEZEBEL'S, CHAPTERS 38–9

Summary

- At Jezebel's, Moira tells Offred about her failed escape attempt from the Red Centre and how she came to be working in the brothel.
- Offred reflects on Moira's unfinished story, celebrating her heroism and the bravery of all the people who helped her.
- In a bedroom at Jezebel's, the Commander takes Offred upstairs for what he assumes will be a pleasurable sexual encounter for them both, but it is doomed to failure and Offred describes herself as lying there 'like a dead bird' (p. 267).

KEY CONTEXT   A03

The 'Whore of Babylon' (p. 254) is a reference to the figure in the Bible who represents Evil or Sin and rides on the back of the beast of Death, with its seven heads and ten horns, in the Apocalypse. See Revelation 17:3–5.

Analysis

Offred and the Commander

Moira suggests in Chapter 38 that the Commander brought Offred to Jezebel's as part of a male power fantasy, and there is plenty of evidence for this feminist analysis. No private relationship between Offred and the Commander is possible, for the personal has become inescapably political. Offred cannot forget that the Commander represents the tyrannical power which is responsible for her losses and that she is his slave, emphasised by her self-admonishment in Chapter 39: 'Bestir yourself. Move your flesh around, breathe audibly. It's the least you can do' (p. 267). She does not want to see him as a naked human being and would prefer the grotesque arrangement with Serena Joy present as well. In bed she feels she has to pretend to enjoy it, both for the Commander's sake and for her own safety, but the encounter is a dismal failure.

Offred's mother

Moira has seen Offred's mother in a film about the Colonies, and when Offred sounds relieved and says 'I thought she was dead' Moira replies darkly that 'She might as well be … You should wish it for her' (p. 264). Offred also remembers in Chapter 39 how she lost contact with her mother and is troubled that she can't remember when she last saw her. In a parallel with the way she likes to think about Moira, Offred finds herself hoping that her mother's 'cockiness, her optimism and energy, her pizzazz, will get her out of this' (p. 265), but fears that her mother's situation is in truth a hopeless one.

KEY CONNECTION   A05

The 'Underground Femaleroad' (p. 258) is an allusion to the Underground Railroad, which was an escape route for runaway slaves from the United States to Canada between 1840 and 1860, prior to the abolition of slavery after the American Civil War. It was an informal network of safe houses and supportive people. Around 30,000 slaves reached Canada in this way.

Study focus: Moira's story

In Chapter 38, notice how Offred embeds the story of Moira's escape attempt inside her own **narrative**, partly to celebrate Moira's heroism and that of all the people who helped her get as far as the Canadian border, and partly as an **elegy** to Moira, who Offred will never see again after tonight. Offred takes trouble to record Moira's story as carefully and accurately as possible, to give her friend a voice: 'I've tried to make it sound as much like her as I can' (p. 256). The sad truth is that Moira has not managed to escape from Gilead any more than Offred's unknown predecessor could, though Offred wishes at the end of the chapter that she could end Moira's story 'with something daring and spectacular, some outrage, something that would befit her' (p. 262). The most that Offred can do if she survives is to tell these stories of heroic resistance.

SECTION XIII NIGHT, CHAPTER 40 & SECTION XIV SALVAGING, CHAPTER 41

Summary

- Offred has her first sexual encounter with Nick.
- Offred falls in love with Nick and their dangerous love affair defies Gileadean tyranny.
- She tells Nick that she believes she is pregnant with his baby. For the first time, Offred wants to stay in Gilead.

Analysis

Multiple retellings

Although she knows she is still being used, this time by the Commander's Wife, Offred's encounter with Nick carries great meaning for Offred. However, her account of their first lovemaking is curiously reticent. She describes their first sexual encounter in three different ways, but she admits that none of them is true because no language can adequately describe the complex experience of falling in love. These multiple versions are also a reminder of Offred's **self-consciousness** as a **narrator**, who creates different effects through her way of telling the story.

In this precarious situation, there is for Offred the further problem of her infidelity to Luke – 'Day by day, night by night he recedes, and I become more faithless' (p. 281) – and her ignorance about his fate. This is all part of the dilemma of human love explored by Offred in her **narrative** as she tries to maintain her integrity in the face of uncertainty, deprivation, desire and mounting danger.

Risk and danger

Atwood illustrates the dangers of disobeying the law in Gilead in the most dramatic and brutal way in this section. By locating Offred's illicit love affair with Nick in 'Salvaging' – the most gruesome section of the novel – (see the Extract Analysis that follows), Atwood underlines the precariousness of their love. Offred is totally compromised not only in relation to her memories of Luke, but also in her official relationship with the Commander and her unofficial relationship with Ofglen's resistance movement. She is also in danger of being shot by mistake in the dark.

Study focus: Offred and Nick

Make sure you can write about how the love scenes with Nick are presented as both ambiguous and tender. To Offred, being in love again is like a refuge in the wilderness, and she abandons herself to this crucial human emotion that Gilead cannot erase. She shows how much she trusts Nick by telling him her real name. For the first time she actually wants to stay in Gilead, as long as she can be with Nick, and she takes many risks to be with him.

A01 PROGRESS BOOSTER

How does the love story between Offred and Nick both conform to and **parody** the conventional 'romance' plot?

EXTRACT ANALYSIS: CHAPTER 41, PAGES 279–80

This fourteenth section of the novel – 'Salvaging' – comes near the novel's end and this extract is taken from its very beginning. The section as a whole depicts particularly brutal and shocking violence perpetrated by the Republic of Gilead against its own citizens. Intertwined with these accounts is Offred's parallel private story not only of bearing witness to these atrocities but also of her attempts to survive them and, increasingly, to experience love.

If the preceding passages for analysis were concerned with 'writing the body', this last one might be described as writing the story as if it were a body. Offred begins by apologising to her readers (or listeners), reminding us of her own compromised situation, acknowledging the suffering and painful conditions out of which her **narrative** is told. Though she light-heartedly remarks on her attempts to lighten her story by making way for pleasant and diverting subjects such as 'sunsets' and 'snow' (p. 279) and indirectly refers to her new love relationship with Nick, her main emphasis is on the misery of her condition, with its boredom and its dangers.

Offred likens the structure of her 'fragmented' story to a dismembered body, using **personification** to portray her story as 'a body caught in crossfire or pulled apart by force' (p. 279). This violent imagery and the use of personification enable her to draw a clear parallel between the victims of the 'salvaging' and 'particicution' and her story, implying that her attempt to give as truthful an account of her experiences in Gilead as possible is itself shaped by the harsh conditions imposed on communication under the Gilead regime. This is one of several points in the novel when Offred draws attention to her account's limitations, partiality and re-constructed nature. As Coral Ann Howells states in *Margaret Atwood* (1996), 'Offred ... shared the postmodern narrator's self-awareness of the dimensions of fabrication in her memoir'. There is also an ironic suggestion that while retelling is on the one hand a survival strategy for Offred, it is also a deeply painful experience: 'Nevertheless it hurts me to tell it over, over again' (p. 279).

KEY INTERPRETATION (A05)

In *The Cambridge Introduction to Margaret Atwood* (2010), Heidi Slettedahl Macpherson writes of Offred that 'she is *not heroic*. She is, instead, a passive everywoman, awaiting rescue ...'

As a **self-conscious narrator**, Offred is aware of her 'limping and mutilated' (p. 279) narrative with its fragmented structure, its isolated scenic units, its gaps and blanks, its dislocated time sequence, and her own hesitations and doubts. Her story is an eyewitness account of disaster, but it is also, as she recognises, a substitute for dialogue and an escape fantasy. Throughout Offred's storytelling process, she has invented her listeners and attempted to believe in their existence: 'By telling you anything at all I'm at least believing in you' (p. 279) – such is her fundamental need to gesture towards a world outside Gilead.

Offred's awareness of her strategy is plain in her deliberate address to readers as 'you' – outside the text and outside Gilead. This is emphasised by her punning variant on Descartes's famous sentence 'I think, therefore I am' into 'I tell, therefore you are' (p. 279). Offred shifts the emphasis from an examination of the enclosed self to speaking about language and communication between human beings, setting up an interaction between an 'I' and a 'you'. Her prison narrative is presented as the only way of bridging the gap between an isolated self and the world outside. Storytelling becomes her means of personal survival, a reconstruction of events and also a way of reconstructing her life after the traumatic disruption of her former existence.

Offred's is indeed a narrative of resistance, challenging not only Gilead's perspective but also the misrepresentations of her experience in the future, for it illustrates the difference between a woman's private narrative of memory and the grand impersonal narrative of history. Offred admits to flaws and failings in herself and in her story, since the two are inseparable, wishing herself 'more active, less hesitant, less distracted by trivia' (p. 279). Having heard Offred's voice, we are unlikely to accept Professor Pieixoto's scholarly gloss in the 'Historical Notes', which consigns her, like Eurydice, to the world of the dead – or at best to the world of romantic myth. At one point in the 'Historical Notes', he pompously refers to her narrative as 'This item – I hesitate to use the word *document*' (p. 313), a description of her testimony that is reductive and silencing. We may not know her future but we do understand her present situation much better than the professor is willing to admit.

Perhaps the crucial point is that despite all her breaks and hesitations, Offred insists on telling her story to her unknown listeners: 'So I will myself to go on' (p. 280). She tells her story in secret and in defiance of a regime that demands total silence and submission from its Handmaids. Ultimately, her story survives the demise of Gilead and exceeds the limits that Gilead tried to impose.

(A03) KEY CONNECTION

In the 'Historical Notes', the Professor likens Offred to Eurydice, who in Greek mythology was the wife of Orpheus. He rescued her from Hades, but when he looked back to see if she was following, she vanished forever. As readers, we may well object to this somewhat reductive and depersonalising judgement on Offred and her testimony. See also Atwood's poems 'Orpheus 1' and 'Orpheus 2', and 'Eurydice', first published in 1984 and collected in her *Eating Fire: Selected Poetry 1965–1995*.

(A01) PROGRESS BOOSTER

Look for examples elsewhere in the novel of Offred imagining that her story has – or will have – an audience, and of how difficult it is for her to go on believing this.

Revision task 8: Remembering and forgetting (A02)

Make notes on the relative importance of remembering and forgetting in Offred's narrative. For example, consider:

- The role played by memories of 'the time before'
- The fragmented nature of Offred's narrative.

SECTION XIV SALVAGING, CHAPTERS 42–4

Summary

- At the Salvaging two Handmaids and one Wife are publicly hanged. Offred cannot look.
- At a Particicution, a man accused of rape is torn to pieces by a mob of outraged Handmaids. Ofglen tells Offred that he was no rapist, but a dissenter like themselves.
- Janine appears with a smear of blood across her cheek and holding a clump of the murdered man's hair tightly in her right hand. According to Offred she is 'in free fall' (p. 292), and is steadily losing her grip on reality.
- Offred's normal life is shattered by the disappearance of the old Ofglen. Ofglen's replacement tells her that her friend hanged herself because she saw the black van coming for her.

Analysis

The Salvaging

The Salvaging is another compulsory outing. Set outside on the lawn in front of what was once the university library, it reminds Offred of a graduation ceremony until the proceedings begin. It is not, however, even a show trial, for the women are hanged for unspecified crimes. It is a frightening display of fanaticism, presided over by Aunt Lydia, in which all Handmaids are forced to become collaborators, for they all have to put their hands on the hanging rope to signify their assent to these killings. The name 'Salvaging' has associations with 'salvage', 'salvation' and 'savage'. However, in a startling example of the abuse of language, the word 'salvaging' came to mean an extra-judicial execution in the Philippines, a point Professor Pieixoto makes in the 'Historical Notes'.

A brutal climax

In this section, Atwood shows us the brutalising effects of crowd hysteria, especially in Chapter 43 when the Salvaging reaches a horrendous climax in the public slaughter of the man supposed to have been convicted of rape. This 'Particicution' (p. 290) is a dreadful spectacle of violence, for it is the Handmaids who are encouraged to kill and dismember him. It is conducted by Aunt Lydia, who blows a whistle as in a football game. Everyone is overcome by a wave of hysteria and revenge, though Offred notices that the man tries to smile and to deny the charge. Ofglen rushes forward and kicks the man to knock him out before he is torn to pieces, and the chapter ends with Ofglen telling Offred that the man was not a rapist but a member of the resistance movement. Through this episode, Atwood shows us the power of the mob, but ultimately these events only underline the power of the Gileadean regime to fuel the mob's anger with a fabricated story about the man's crimes, and make him a scapegoat.

Key quotation: *'I am, I am. I am, still'* **A02**

Offred's own reaction to the Particicution makes her extremely uncomfortable, for the man's terrible death has acted on her like a stimulant, enhancing her own hunger to survive. With striking honesty, she declares at the end of Chapter 43 that she is 'hungry' and that 'This is monstrous, but nevertheless it's true' (p. 293). She concludes that it might be 'the body's way of seeing to it that I remain alive, continue to repeat its bedrock prayer: *I am, I am*. I am, still' (p. 293).

SECTION XIV SALVAGING, CHAPTER 45 & SECTION XV NIGHT, CHAPTER 46

SUMMARY

- The knowledge that Ofglen committed suicide before she could be made to confess and endanger her comrades brings Offred to a point where she feels for the first time that she has been defeated and overpowered by Gilead.
- Serena Joy confronts Offred with a more personal betrayal, holding out evidence of her secret evening out with the Commander. She also tells Offred that she will meet the same fate as her predecessor.
- Offred feels overwhelmed by fatigue and despair, and just at this moment hears the siren of a black van coming to the house. She fears that Nick has betrayed her.
- She expects a stranger to enter her room but it is Nick. She wonders whether he is a 'private Eye' (p. 305), but he whispers that this is Mayday come to her rescue, and more significantly he calls her by her real name.
- Offred departs from the Commander's house, escorted out by the Eyes like a criminal.

Analysis

Offred's fate

At the end of Chapter 46, Offred has no idea whether she is about to go to prison or to freedom, but she allows herself to be helped up into the van. Nick's use of Offred's real name on page 305 – a secret which Offred told him during their lovemaking – would seem to be a coded message of reassurance to Offred and to the reader, as is his mention of the word 'Mayday'. In the midst of her uncertainty and powerlessness, it is a final gesture of trust and faith, confirmed by the ambiguous final words of the novel 'And so I step up, into the darkness within; or else the light' (p. 307).

Study focus: A twist in the tale   **A02**

These final chapters of Offred's **narrative** are full of unexpected twists and turns. Offred's decision to stop fighting the regime in Chapter 45 brings with it a feeling of relief, only for this to be snatched away by the Wife's revelation. The plot now gathers pace; it seems to be moving towards a **denouement**. Offred sits in her room at the beginning of Chapter 46, 'waiting' (p. 303). She considers a variety of possible escapes, but says she considers these things 'idly' (p. 304) and does nothing. For Offred, this is a moment of total despair as she feels as trapped as her predecessor – 'my ancestress, my double' (p. 305) – whose defiance ended in suicide.

Then comes a break in the text and an astonishing intervention, for suddenly Offred hears the siren of the black van and a group of Eyes led by Nick push open her door. The dramatic events of the last few pages of Offred's narrative describe Offred's exit from the house and from her story as we know it, leaving her fate both uncertain and untold.

A03 KEY CONTEXT

The coming of the van and the uncertainty of Offred's destination are echoes of life in real totalitarian regimes, from Stalinist Russia and Nazi Germany to apartheid in South Africa and the 'disappearances' under the military juntas of Chile and Argentina.

A04 KEY CONNECTION

Things to Come (1936) scripted by H.G. Wells is the classic futuristic **dystopia**, offering a masculine perspective on history which is vast and chilling.

HISTORICAL NOTES ON *THE HANDMAID'S TALE*

Summary

- The novel shifts to AD 2195. Gilead is in ruins and all the previous **protagonists** are dead. At a conference, a session is being chaired by Professor Crescent Moon.
- We learn how Offred's story has survived and why its structure is so fragmented. It was not written down but recorded on cassette tapes that were transcribed.
- Professor Pieixoto, from Cambridge University, explains how it has been impossible to definitively identify the true identities of Offred, the Commander, Serena Joy and the others, though he suggests possible theories.

Analysis

Pieixoto's scholarship

This is the last 'reconstruction' of Offred's tale, and in itself it is a sharply **satirical** attack on academic methods and manners. Atwood encourages the reader to laugh or groan along with Pieixoto's audience as he jokes at the opening of his talk about the meanings of the words 'enjoy', 'tale'/'tail' and '"The Underground Femaleroad," since dubbed by some of our historical wags "The Underground Frailroad." *(Laughter, groans.)'* (p. 313). If we see *The Handmaid's Tale* as a letter, it is Pieixoto who finally delivers the message to a wide audience, transforming 'her-story' into 'history' (or 'his-story') in the process. But for all Pieixoto's scholarship, he cannot get beyond generalities, and fails to tell us what we most want to know as readers of a gripping and troubling novel: what happened to Offred. We may also feel that there is an uneasy juxtaposition between the 'objective' view of history pursued by Pieixoto – 'Our job is not to censure but to understand' (p. 315) – and the personal and painful account by Offred of the hardship and atrocities she had to endure in 'Early Gilead' (p. 321).

Progress booster: A new perspective

When writing about the 'Historical Notes' make sure you can discuss how they provide a framework for looking back at Offred's **narrative** from a distant point in the future. Serving as a kind of epilogue to the story, Atwood's 'Historical Notes' give a different perspective on Offred, for here she is no longer a living, suffering human being but an elusive anonymous voice whose story is nothing more than a historical anecdote. It is also a view from outside the United States, for this paper is being given in Arctic Canada by an archival historian from the University of Cambridge, England. Offred's fate remains a mystery and the final question invites us as readers to participate in interpreting the multiple and contradictory meanings of the novel.

Key quotation: Offred's tale A01

Professor Pieixoto criticises Offred's account: 'She could have told us much about the workings of the Gileadean empire, had she had the instincts of a reporter or a spy' (p. 322). Offred does have these instincts, but chooses to report on private matters, providing a **counter-discourse** which challenges Gilead's **patriarchal narrative**. This is one of several points in Pieixoto's talk where we may feel that his historical interpretation misses the point. However we may be thankful for his scholarly endeavours as, through them, her tale has survived, so that now at last Offred can speak for herself.

PROGRESS CHECK

Section One: Check your understanding

These tasks will help you to evaluate your knowledge and skills level in this particular area.

1.   Compile a glossary of terms used in Gilead, for example *Ceremony, Computalk* and *Econowife*.

2.   List four or five moments in the text that show Offred at her most defiant, and comment briefly on the significance of each.

3.   What do we learn about Offred's life and family before Gilead? Make a list.

4.   How is the feminist movement of the 1970s presented in the text? Write a paragraph summarising your thoughts.

5.   Make notes on three violent events that take place in *The Handmaid's Tale*.

6.   In which chapters do we learn about Ofwarren/Janine? Write a paragraph about her various appearances.

7.   What is the narrative function of the 'Night' sections?

8.   What is the significance of Offred's account of the prayers in the sitting room before the Ceremony takes place, as described in Chapters 14 and 15?

9.   What do we learn about life in Gilead in the accounts of Offred and Ofglen's shopping trips? Make a list.

10.   List four or five moments that shed light on the character of the Commander and his role in the text. Briefly describe that role.

11.   What is the narrative function of Offred's predecessor – the Commander's previous Handmaid 'Offred'? Write a paragraph explaining your ideas.

12.   Identify where in the text we learn about the Handmaids' 're-education' for their new role, and make notes about what we learn about this process.

13.   What is the signficance of the episodes that take place in the garden? Make a list.

14.   How does Atwood introduce and develop the idea of an underground resistance movement in Gilead? Write a timeline showing what is revealed and when.

15.   How does Offred write about her body? Write a paragraph discussing your evidence and ideas.

16.   What is the significance to the text as a whole of Offred's visit to Jezebel's? Make brief notes.

17.   List three moments where Offred questions her own version of events as a narrator. What is the effect of these moments on the reader?

18.   Write a paragraph outlining what we know about the relationship between Offred and Nick.

19.   What do you find striking about the way Atwood presents Offred's exit from the house in Chapter 46?

20.   What do the 'Historical Notes' contribute? Write a paragraph summarising your thoughts.

Section Two: Working towards the exam

Below are five tasks which require longer, more developed answers. In each case, read the question carefully, select the key areas you need to address, and plan an essay of six to seven points. Write a first draft, giving yourself an hour to do so. Make sure you include supporting evidence for each point, including quotations.

1. *'The Handmaid's Tale* is a survival narrative.' Discuss.
2. Consider the role of memory in this novel.
3. What do we learn about the narrator from the way she tells and structures her story?
4. To what extent is Atwood's novel a love story?
5. Choose three characters and write about the different ways in which they are shown by Atwood to be victims of the system in Gilead.

Progress check (rate your understanding on a level of 1 – low, to 5 – high)	1	2	3	4	5
The significance of particular events and how they relate to each other					
How the major and minor characters contribute to the action					
How Atwood uses the device of the narrator					
How Atwood structures the novel					
What we know about the story's outcome and how this affects our view of the protagonists					

CHARACTERS

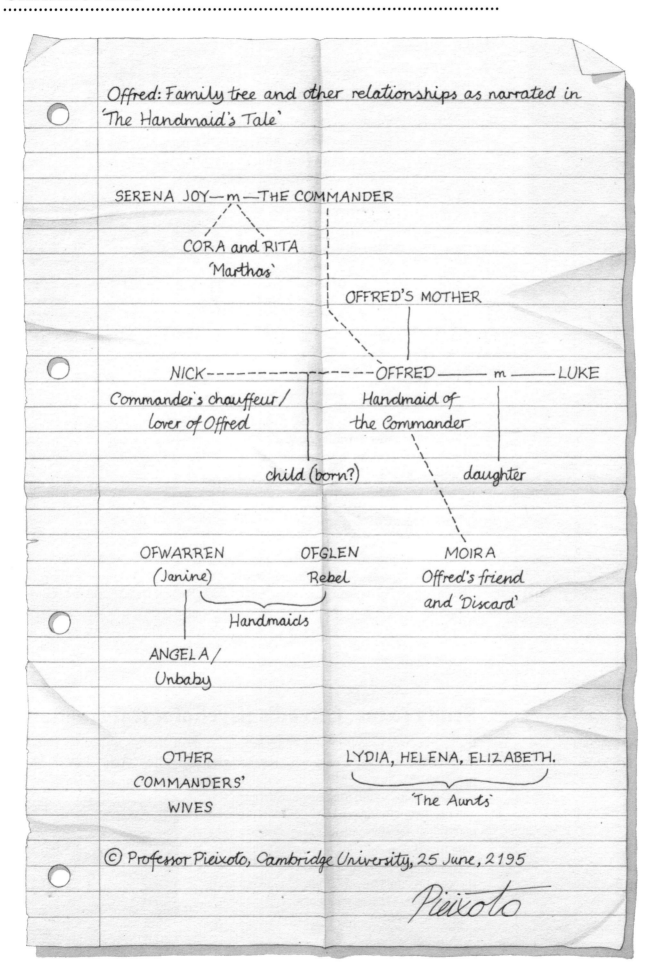

Offred: Family tree and other relationships as narrated in 'The Handmaid's Tale'

SERENA JOY—m—THE COMMANDER

CORA and RITA
'Marthas'

OFFRED'S MOTHER

NICK- - - - - - - - - - - - -OFFRED——— m ———LUKE

Commander's chauffeur/
lover of Offred

Handmaid of
the Commander

child (born?)   daughter

OFWARREN   OFGLEN   MOIRA

(Janine)   Rebel   Offred's friend
and 'Discard'

Handmaids

ANGELA/
Unbaby

OTHER   LYDIA, HELENA, ELIZABETH.

COMMANDERS'

WIVES   'The Aunts'

© Professor Pieixoto, Cambridge University, 25 June, 2195

Pieixoto

Offred

Who is Offred?

- The main **protagonist** and narrator, Offred is a young woman who is trapped in Gilead as a Handmaid, a form of surrogate mother/servant.
- She was once married to Luke, and had a child.
- The name she is known by, Of-fred, is derived from the name of her current Commander – she does not reveal her former, real name.
- She is a survivor from the past who uses memories of her husband and child to help her carry on in the present.

The function of a Handmaid

Under the terms of the totalitarian Gileadean state, Offred's individuality is erased and replaced with the status of generic woman-for-breeding – she is one of the 'two-legged wombs' (p. 146). She is denied all her individual rights – her fate is to be virtually imprisoned in the domestic spaces of the home and only allowed out with a shopping partner and for Handmaids' official excursions like Prayvaganzas and Salvagings. Most of the time she is isolated and afraid.

At the age of thirty-three and potentially still fertile, she is a victim of Gileadean sexist **ideology** which equates 'male' with power and sexual potency, and 'female' with submission and reproduction. In her **narrative**, however, Offred resists being reduced in this way: she refuses to forget her past or her own name when she was a daughter, lover, wife, working mother and friend. She refuses to give up hope of escape.

The significance of a name

Offred's identity as an individual has been erased and she has been forbidden to use her own name. She keeps it, however like a buried treasure, as a guarantee of her other identity: 'I keep the knowledge of this name like something hidden, some treasure I'll come back to dig up, one day' (p. 94). She gives her real name as a love token to Nick, and he in turn uses it as an exchange of trust when he comes for her with the black van: 'He calls me by my real name. Why should this mean anything?' (p. 305). Offred does not trust the reader with her real name, however, which is a sign of her fear in a dangerous situation.

PROGRESS BOOSTER A02

Consider in what ways Offred's tale can be thought of as a resistance narrative. Weigh up the evidence for and against – for example, Offred is neither a member of Mayday nor an obvious social dissident. How might her narrative seek to undermine the totalitarian regime she is now subject to?

Study focus: Offred's psychological freedom A02

It is important to be able to write about how Offred retains her psychological freedom. She is a survivor from the past, and it is her power to remember which helps her to cope in the present. She reconstructs the past through **flashbacks** (these are her most effective escape routes from isolation, loneliness and boredom). The layered image of past and present her narrative provides in Chapter 1 is like a **palimpsest** (a manuscript where later writing has been superimposed on earlier, erased words). Offred succeeds in simultaneously inhabiting two spaces: her Handmaid's space (or lack of it), and the freer, happier spaces of memory.

Offred's lively curiosity

An attractive characteristic of Offred is her lively responsiveness to the world around her. She is sharply observant of physical details in her surroundings. She is curious and likes to explore. Her response to the Commander's Wife's beautiful garden is emotional, even poetic. She notes all its seasonal changes in detail, for it represents for her all the healthy growth and fertility of the natural world. These things are denied by the regime, but outside the window the beauty of the garden flourishes.

Her observations about the garden reveal her resistance to the regime: 'There is something subversive about this garden of Serena's, a sense of buried things bursting upwards, wordlessly, into the light' (p. 161). Her response to the moon is also poetic: 'a wishing moon, a sliver of ancient rock, a goddess, a wink. The moon is a stone and the sky is full of deadly hardware, but oh God, how beautiful anyway' (p. 108). This ironic observation is typical of Offred's character and reveals her refusal to give up on life.

Subversion versus rebellion

Offred's attitude is discreetly subversive but never openly rebellious. She watches for those moments of instability which she calls 'tiny peepholes' (p. 31) when human responses break through official surfaces. It is this sharpness of mind which informs her mischievous, critical view of her present situation, as in the satisfaction she gets out of teasing the young guard at the gate: 'I enjoy the power; power of a dog bone, passive but there' (p. 32).

She consistently refuses to be deceived by the **rhetoric** of Gilead, for she believes in the value of every individual. Of the men in her life, she says: 'Each one remains unique, there is no way of joining them together. They cannot be exchanged, one for the other. They cannot replace each other' (pp. 201–2). She yearns for communication and trust between people instead of mutual suspicion and isolation.

Ironically, Offred's fullest human relationship in Gilead is her 'arrangement' with the Commander: 'The fact is that I'm his mistress' (p. 172). This is where 'taboo dissolved' (p. 165), for it is in their Scrabble games that Offred is at her liveliest and her most conventionally feminine. In his study, Offred and the Commander relate to each other by old familiar social and sexual codes, which eases the loneliness both feel. It is after her first evening that Offred does something she has never done before in the novel: she laughs out loud, partly at the absurdity of it all, but partly out of a reawakening of her own high spirits. Yet she is too intelligent ever to forget that it is only a game or a **parody** of the past, and her outing to Jezebel's confirms this. For all its glitter, her purple sequinned costume, like the evening, is a shabby masquerade, and in the clear light of day she is left sitting with 'a handful of crumpled stars' in her lap (p. 303).

 PROGRESS BOOSTER

'I've tried to put some of the good things in as well. Flowers, for instance' (p. 279). Examine Offred's vocabulary of images, in the light of her statement. The use of natural imagery contrasts with the polluted, technological world of Gilead and so Offred's **narrative** can be viewed as feminine subversion in a male-dominated world.

Progress booster: Offred's model of resistance

A05

It is important to keep in mind that *The Handmaid's Tale* is **dystopian** fiction. Political and/or social comment, driven by the need or want for change, can be in many ways more important than the characters, and through them Atwood may present us with models of an ideological position. Consider what kind of model complex characters such as Offred and Moira offer. For example, Offred's model of resistance is to work surreptitiously, while Moira is more confrontational. Another way to think of this is in terms of the contrast between moderate political resistance and direct action.

Hope for the future

Offred succeeds in finding new hope for the future in her relationship with Nick. Her first encounter with him is in the dark, where fear and sexual risk exert a powerful charge which runs through the novel to its end. Their love represents the forbidden combination of desire and rebellion – living in a terrorist state, she must always be on her alert to the glint of danger. Being with Nick allows Offred to hope; she even comes to terms with her new, reduced circumstances in the present. Like a pioneer who has given up the Old World and come to the wilderness of a new one, she says: 'I have made a life for myself, here, of a sort. That must have been what the settlers' wives thought' (p. 283).

Offred's detailed psychological narrative shows how she can survive loss and bereavement. It also shows how she manages to evade and find ways to challenge the absolute authority of the state. Her narrative reveals her feelings, her state of mind and her wry sense of humour. She is a highly **self-conscious** narrator who is aware of her own contradictions and failings. She knows she lacks Moira's flamboyant courage. She accuses herself of being a coward, and unreliable. At the end, she feels guilty for having betrayed the members of the household who imprisoned her.

Despite Offred's own self-doubt, we are convinced of her integrity – she keeps her dignity and self-respect as she embraces the possibility of escape with hope. She is a different kind of heroine: one who wins the battle against the numbing boredom of her existence; who deals with the everyday practicalities of a life where there is so much danger. Her narrative represents the freedom and resilience of the human spirit. She lingers in the reader's memory like 'a wraith of red smoke' (p. 219).

KEY INTERPRETATION (A05)

The author's own comment throws light on Offred's detailed psychological narrative. Atwood said: 'You're dealing with a character whose ability to move in the society was limited. She was boxed in … the more limited and boxed in you are, the more important details become. If you are in jail in solitary, the advent of a rat can be pretty important to you.' See *Margaret Atwood, Conversations*, p. 216.

Key quotation: A moment of laughter but no way out

On page 156 Offred says, 'there's no way out of here'. She has experienced a moment of apparent freedom in her laughing fit, yet finally she is reminded that she is trapped – her world closes in; all senses are reduced to leave only the rhythm of her heart. Her 'attack' of mirth is presented as disturbing, like 'an epileptic fit'. Offred chokes, she hurts as the laughter boils in her throat. Viewed this way, the episode becomes a moment of **pathos** – a poignant reminder of her loneliness and isolation. Offred can laugh, but she can make no sound.

Moira

Who is Moira?

- Moira is Offred's oldest friend and a survivor of the permissive society that existed before Gilead.
- Moira is a spirited rebel; she is a 'Discard', consigned to the brothel.

A female rebel

Moira, always known by her own name because she never becomes a Handmaid, is strongly individual. We can view her role in the novel as that of an openly declared lesbian. This is a position which can be viewed in two ways: from Offred's point of view Moira is the embodiment of female heroism. From the Gileadean authorities' point of view she is a 'loose woman', a criminal element, and her story follows the conventional fictional pattern of such rebellious figures: when Offred last sees her she is working as a prostitute in Jezebel's. Even here, Moira manages to express her protest against the regime. She remains a declared lesbian and her sexually provocative 'Bunny Girl' costume is absurd and deliberately distorted. The costume is 'Government issue' (p. 254), and Moira's own wryly comic comment on its suitability for her is, 'I guess they thought it was me'; the idea that 'they' might consider a Bunny Girl outfit appropriate for Moira's character is one we may find comic, yet endearing and full of pathos.

Speaking out

In the pre-Gileadean American permissive society, Moira was a non-conformist, fashionable college student who wore purple overalls and left her unfinished paper on 'Date rape' (p. 47) to go to the bar. Much more astute about sexual politics than Offred, she was an activist in the Gay Rights movement, working for a women's collective at the time of the Gilead coup. When she is brought into the Rachel and Leah Centre she is still wearing jeans and declares that the place is a 'loony bin' (p. 81).

Despite Moira's rebelliousness, the sad fact is that she and outspoken women like her are sent off to the Colonies or commit suicide, which Offred herself refuses to do. Atwood presents both Offred and Moira as feminist heroines, showing women's energetic resistance to the Gilead system, but there are no winners here. Neither compromise nor rebellion wins freedom, though it is likely that Offred is rescued by Nick. However, they do challenge the tyranny and oppression of the Gileadean state. Their value lies in their speaking out against the conditions of silence that are imposed upon them. Their stories highlight the actions of two individual women whose very different private beliefs become **symbolic** as ideals for others to follow. Their voices survive as images of hope and defiance to be vindicated by history.

Study focus: Moira's outfit as grotesque ⓐ⓪⑤

Look closely at Moira's clothing at Jezebel's. She is 'dressed absurdly' (p. 250) in an outfit that distorts her breasts, wearing misshapen rabbit ears. Like the others, she no doubt wears 'clownish' (p. 247) make-up which distorts the faces of the prostitutes, making their eyes 'too big', 'too dark and shimmering, their mouths too red, too wet'. We can view this as **grotesque**: it is both comic and repugnant, frightening even. How do the distorted, exaggerated images of the women make us as readers feel about Offred and Moira? Their final meeting is one with **comic** elements but it is also a moment of horror and sadness at what they have become.

Ⓐ⓪③ KEY CONTEXT

In Atwood's critical history of North American feminism, Moira represents the 'individualistic' models of feminism of the late 1980s and 1990s. These include the different agendas of groups of women who were previously marginalised in society: black women and lesbians whose interests are closer to Gay Rights than to traditionally liberal feminist agendas of an earlier generation.

Ⓐ⓪③ KEY INTERPRETATION

Lee Briscoe Thompson in *Scarlet Letters* describes Moira as Offred's 'rebel alter ego' (p. 39), highlighting the contrast between two types of female heroism. Offred practises rebellion through subversion and independence of thought. She does not dare do more. Moira's escape is active rebellion, which leads to the beatings that she endures. Both are courageous, in their separate ways. Offred may, finally, make her escape – but ironically perhaps, Moira is reduced to subversive behaviour. All that remains to her is the unregistered protest of her bizarre brothel outfit – and her journey to the Colonies.

Serena Joy

Who is Serena Joy?

- Serena Joy is the Commander's Wife with power over Offred.
- Elderly and childless, she has had to agree to take in a Handmaid.
- In her former life Serena Joy was a child singing star, then a media personality.

A powerful female presence

Serena Joy, the Commander's Wife, is the most powerful female presence in Offred's daily life in Gilead. Offred has plenty of opportunity to observe her at close quarters, and so she appears in the **narrative** as more than just a member of a class in the hierarchy of Gileadean women. Significantly, unlike all the other Wives, she is referred to by her own name.

As an elderly, childless woman she has to agree to the grotesque system of polygamy (where a husband may take more than one wife) practised in Gilead and to shelter a Handmaid in her home. It is plain, however, that she resents this arrangement keenly. It is a violation of her marriage, and a continual reminder of the way she is deteriorating physically (she suffers from arthritis and uses a cane to walk) and her own fading looks.

A celebrity in her former life

The irony of the situation is made clear when Offred remembers Serena Joy's past history. Serena Joy was a child singing star on a gospel television show. Later she was a media personality. She spoke out for extreme conservative domestic policies which supported the idea that women's rightful place was in the home. Now, as Offred maliciously remarks, Serena is trapped in the very **ideology** on which she had based her popularity: 'She stays in her home, but it doesn't seem to agree with her' (p. 56).

A parody of the virtuous woman

Serena's present life is a **parody** of the Virtuous Woman (In the Old Testament of the Bible, a Virtuous Woman is described as one who is content to be ruled by her husband and who always puts his needs first). Her only place of power is her own living room. She is estranged from her husband, jealous of her Handmaid, and has nothing to do except knit scarves for soldiers and gossip with acquaintances, or listen to her young voice on the gramophone. The only space for Serena's self-expression is her garden, and even that she cannot tend without the help of her husband's chauffeur. If flowers are important to Offred, so too are they to Serena. She often sits alone in her 'subversive garden' (p. 161), knitting or smoking or viciously cutting off the heads of flowers.

Study focus: Serena Joy described

A01

On page 25 Serena Joy says to Offred, 'I want to see as little of you as possible'. Look closely at the descriptions of Serena Joy; while we never really know what Offred looks like, Serena Joy's face is described in close detail. Through Offred's observations, we also learn how Serena Joy moves; how she spends her time and how difficult she, too, finds the copulation ceremonies. In what ways is she a significant presence in the novel?

KEY CONTEXT **A03**

Serena Joy is a **satirical** portrait, made up of several Christian Right wives who were media personalities in the early 1980s: Tammy Faye Bakker, who with her husband ran a gospel television show; Phyllis Schlafly, a lawyer who campaigned for women's return to the home; and Beverley LaHaye, who organised demonstrations against abortions and the Equal Rights Amendment (ERA).

Serena Joy's attitudes and tastes

Offred seldom knows what Serena is thinking, though there are indications of her attitudes and tastes in the jewels and the perfume she wears and in the furnishings of her house: 'hard lust for quality, soft sentimental cravings', as Offred uncharitably puts it (p. 90). Serena is very possessive of the Commander: 'As for my husband … he's just that. My husband. I want that to be perfectly clear. Till death do us part. It's final' (p. 26). There is also evidence of a certain toughness in Serena's cigarette smoking and her use of slang, not to mention her suggestion that Offred, unknown to the Commander, should sleep with Nick in order to conceive the child she is supposed to produce: 'She's actually smiling, coquettishly even; there's a hint of her former small-screen mannequin's allure, flickering over her face like momentary static' (p. 216). But Serena has her revenges too: she has deliberately withheld from Offred the news of her lost daughter and the photograph of her for which Offred has been longing.

Study focus: A love triangle **A01**

Notice how Serena Joy is one of the points in the triangular relationship which develops between Offred and the Commander. The Ceremony where Offred is coupled with the Commander is imposed by the Gileadean state rules, but as their relationship develops into something more, it can appear to have elements of a conventional plot about an extra-marital affair, where Serena occupies the role of the wife in a typical love triangle. As Offred comments, 'The fact is that I'm his mistress … Sometimes I think she knows' (p. 172). Actually, Serena Joy does not know until she finds the purple costume and the lipstick on Offred's cloak. It is a clichéd situation, but Serena's own pain of loss seems to go beyond the usual story of marital betrayal: '"Behind my back," she says. "You could have left me something."' Offred wonders, 'Does she love him, after all?' (p. 299). On Offred's departure, Serena's last offensive comment, '"After all he did for you"' (p. 307) contains none of the usual pieties of Gilead. It is more a 'wifely' comment from a bygone era.

Key quotation: Doubling **A01**

Offred asks, 'Which of us is it worse for, her or me?' (p. 106); the copulation ceremony is difficult for both Offred and Serena Joy. Offred encourages us to see the world through her eyes alone, but Serena Joy's perspective on some aspects of her life is perhaps similar to Offred's, and seeing the world through her eyes shifts the emphasis of Offred's narrative. They both want a child, and both focus attention on the Commander. In this respect they can be viewed not as opposites but as **doubles**, as conveyed by the balanced quality of the phrase 'her or me?'.

The other Commanders' Wives

Who are the other Commanders' Wives?

- The other Commanders' Wives are members of the upper class in the Gileadean hierarchy.
- They do not exist fully as characters – their lives are mundane, made tolerable by small tasks.

A gaggle of gossips

The other Commanders' Wives exist merely as a gaggle of gossips in blue, for Offred knows nothing of their lives apart from overhearing snatches of their conversation at Birth Days, Prayvaganzas or social visits, when they make scandalous comments about their Handmaids. Only the Wife of Warren achieves a moment of grotesque individuality when she is seen sitting on the Birthing Stool behind Janine, 'wearing white cotton socks, and bedroom slippers, blue ones made of fuzzy material, like toilet-seat covers' (p. 135). There is also one other unfortunate Wife who is hanged at the Salvaging, but Offred does not know what her crime was. Was it murder? Was it adultery? 'It could always be that. Or attempted escape' (p. 287).

Study focus: An ironic image of death

Look closely at the language used at the birth to describe the Wife of Warren. On page 126 she lies on the floor, 'her greying hair spreading like mildew over the rug'. A Birth Day is one where new life is celebrated – but the image here is one of death and decay. Offred mocks her when she comes forward for the birth itself, calling her 'ridiculous' with her 'spindly legs sticking out' (p. 135). Offred says, 'She must know what we think of her'. In this ironic presentation of the Wife as an inanimate object or stuffed toy, we understand her meaning.

The Aunts

Who are the Aunts?

- They are older women, members of a group of collaborators.
- They train and police the Handmaids and deal out punishments.

Female collaborators

Like the Wives, the Marthas, the Econowives and most of the Handmaids, the Aunts are presented as members of a class or group, every group representing a different female role within Gilead.

They are a paramilitary organisation, as is signified by their khaki uniforms and their cattle prods. As propagandists of the regime, they tell distorted tales of women's lives in the pre-Gileadean past. The villainesses of the novel, they are responsible for the most gruesome cruelties, like the female Salvagings and the Particicutions, as well as for individual punishments at the Rachel and Leah Centre.

Ofglen and Ofwarren

Who are Ofglen and Ofwarren?

- Apart from Offred, Ofglen and Ofwarren are the only two Handmaids to emerge as individuals in the novel.
- Ofglen is revealed as fighting the Gileadean state through resistance – she is courageous and rebellious.
- Ofwarren, by contrast, is a conventional female victim figure who gives birth to an 'Unbaby'.
- Both are casualties of the Gileadean system.

Ofglen: a secret life

Ofglen has no past life that Offred knows about, but she does have a secret life as a member of the Mayday resistance movement, which she confides to Offred after weeks as her shopping partner. There is nothing exceptional about her appearance except her mechanical quality, which Offred notices, 'as if she's voice-activated, as if she's on little oiled wheels' (p. 53). Offred is proved right in her suspicions, for under the disguise of Handmaid, Ofglen is a sturdy resistance fighter. She identifies the alleged rapist as 'one of ours' (p. 292) and knocks him out before the horrible Particicution begins. She also dies as a fighter, preferring to commit suicide when she sees the black van coming rather than betray her friends under torture. Offred learns this from her replacement, the 'new, treacherous Ofglen' (p. 297), who whispers the news to her on their shopping expedition.

Study focus: Ofglen as a model of female heroism **A01**

Consider the ways in which Ofglen is presented as strong, for example her proactive behaviour at the Particicution. Examine the way Atwood uses what we might consider 'male', dynamic verbs to describe Ofglen's actions here. Ofglen also steadies Offred when she is in danger of losing control. Moira's attempts to escape show her unquenchable spirit; Ofglen is a fighter. How significant is she in Atwood's representation of female heroism?

Ofwarren (Janine): a victim of the system

Ofwarren/Janine is a female victim in both her lives: before Gilead when she worked as a waitress and was raped by a gang of thugs, then as a Handmaid. At the Rachel and Leah Centre she is presented as a pathetic figure, on the edge of nervous collapse, and consequently one of Aunt Lydia's pets. Though she has her moment of triumph as the 'vastly pregnant' (p. 36) Handmaid Ofwarren in Chapter 5, she is also a victim of the system in which she has tried so hard to curry favour. Even at the Birth Day she is neglected as soon as the baby is born and left 'crying helplessly, burnt-out miserable tears' when her baby is taken away and given to the Wife (p. 137). There is no reward for Janine. Her baby is declared an Unbaby and destroyed because it is deformed; Janine becomes a pale shadow overwhelmed with guilt. Finally, after the Particicution, when Offred sees her again, she has slipped into her own world where she can no longer distinguish fantasy from reality.

A05 **PROGRESS BOOSTER**

Offred says, of Janine, 'What did she ever want but to lead her life as agreeably as possible?' (p. 127).

If Ofglen is a model of female strength, Janine is a victim throughout, and displays weakness, wanting sympathy and support from the Aunts. In the Centre, when she tells the story of her gang-rape in pre-Gileadean times, she is viewed without sympathy, in animalistic terms and is taunted in childlike, playground language: 'Crybaby' (p. 82). In the birthing scene, however, her pain is portrayed unflinchingly. Consider Atwood's portrayal of Ofwarren. Do you think she intends us to feel sympathy for her?

A01 **KEY QUOTATION**

On page 53 Ofglen utters the resistance code word 'It's a beautiful May day', but at this point Offred is unaware of the significance of this, and responds only with the expected 'Praise be'. It is only later (p. 176) that Ofglen reveals herself as a member of the resistance when with Offred she stops at Soul Scrolls, the retail outlet that now does business in prayers. Ofglen's resistance provides a glimmer of hope for Offred's future. But one of the sinister black vans moves in and two 'Eyes' select a man, beat him and bundle him away in the van. The positioning of these two events together reminds us of Offred's danger and ensures that tension levels remain high.

Offred's Mother

Who is Offred's mother?

- In pre-Gileadean times, Offred's mother was a political activist.
- She campaigned for women's sexual and social freedom.
- Offred's mother reappears as a young woman in a film that Offred sees.

A political activist

Offred's mother belongs to the history of feminism that is being recorded in this novel – we are told that she joined the Women's Liberation Movement of the 1960s and 1970s, campaigning for women's sexual and social freedom. As an older woman she continued to be a political activist, and at the time of the Gileadean takeover she disappeared. Only much later does Offred learn that she has been condemned as an 'Unwoman' and sent to the Colonies.

Like Moira, and possessing the same kind of energy, Offred's mother resists classification. In an odd way she even resists being dead, for she makes two startling appearances in the present, both times on film at the Rachel and Leah Centre. On one occasion Offred is shocked to see her as a young woman marching toward her in a pro-choice march. Later Moira reports seeing her as an old woman carrying out slave labour in the Colonies.

Independence of mind

Gradually Offred comes to understand her mother's independence of mind, for she is more than a feminist icon. She haunts her daughter's memory, and Offred admires her courage. As an older woman, she proudly defends her position as a single parent to Offred's husband. At the same time, she accuses her daughter of being naïve and politically irresponsible. It is jaunty language that Offred remembers as distinguishing her mother: 'A man is just a woman's strategy for making other women. Not that your father wasn't a nice guy and all, but he wasn't up to fatherhood. Not that I expected it of him … I said, I make a decent salary, I can afford daycare. So he went to the coast and sent Christmas cards. He had beautiful blue eyes though' (pp. 130–1).

Progress booster: A model of feminism **A02**

Offred can remember a time when she was embarrassed by her mother's activism. She says, 'No mother is ever, completely, a child's idea of what a mother should be' (p. 190); she disapproved of her mother's violence in the abortion riots. Imprisoned in the totalitarian Republic of Gilead, Offred also recalls the underhand and violent ways in which the regime took control. Do we (unlike Offred perhaps) view Offred's mother's militant feminism as heroic, or can we draw difficult parallels between her confrontational, violent methods of opposition and the twisted fundamentalism of the Christian Right under the new regime?

KEY CONTEXT **A03**

Those supporting 'first wave' feminism campaigned for legal, educational and economic rights for women, and in particular the right to vote. 'Second wave' feminism shared these ideals but sought to place women's sexuality and reproduction rights at the centre of political discussion. See Maggie Humm, *Feminisms*, p. 53. Atwood aligns Offred's mother with this later movement.

KEY INTERPRETATION **A05**

Deprived of the freedoms her mother fought for, Offred learns to admire her mother's courage and to value her memory as a vital link with her own lost identity. Her **elegy** to her mother underlines the thematic **motif** of Missing Persons, and particularly lost mothers and daughters, which runs through the novel.

The Commander

Who is the Commander?

- The Commander is the most powerful authority figure in Offred's world, and she takes his first name.
- Despite his position of power, the Commander is presented as a lonely man.

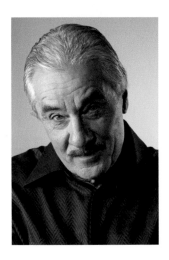

A detailed description

Offred describes the Commander in detail. His high-ranking status means he wears a black uniform and is driven in an impressive car, a 'Whirlwind'. He is an elderly man with 'straight neatly brushed silver hair' and a moustache and blue eyes. He is slightly stooped and 'His manner is mild' (p. 97). As Offred observes him with his gold-rimmed glasses on his nose reading from the Bible before the monthly Ceremony, she thinks he looks 'like a midwestern bank president' (p. 97). This is an astute judgement, as he tells her much later that before Gilead he was in market research (p. 195).

A stereotypical image of male power

The image the Commander presents is that of male power, isolated and benignly indifferent to domestic matters, which include his Wife and his Handmaid. This is, however, not entirely true, for Offred has seen him earlier on the day of the Ceremony, a figure lurking in the shadows outside her room, who tried to peer at her as she passed: 'Something has been shown to me, but what is it?' (p. 59).

The Commander's stereotypical image of male power begins to break down after the official Ceremony. He performs this in full dress uniform and with his eyes closed. It is he who asks Offred to visit him 'after hours' in his study; here, she comes to know him a little more. He is a lonely man who desires friendship and intimacy with his Handmaid and not the serviceable monthly sex for which she has been allocated to him. In his 'Bluebeard's chamber', what he has to offer is not 'kinky sex' but Scrabble games. He seeks an approximation of 'normal life', with conversation, books and magazines. He knows that all of these are forbidden to Handmaids.

Progress booster: A dichotomous relationship (A02)

It is important that you can write about how Atwood explores ideas of power in private and public spheres. Consider the relationship between the Commander and Offred. It exists in secret, behind the door of the Commander's study, and in public, where it is constructed as something very different. In each context the balance of power changes. These two different 'faces' of their relationship can be described as a 'dichotomy' – a division or contrast between two things that are represented as being opposed or entirely different.

(A05) PROGRESS BOOSTER

Notice how the Commander is presented as an ambiguous figure, substantial but shadowy, whose motivations, like his career in Gilead, remain unclear to Offred. Even in the 'Historical Notes' his identity remains uncertain. Why might this be?

(A03) KEY CONTEXT

The Commander's study has echoes of Bluebeard's chamber. In the French folk tale written by Charles Perrault, *Histoires ou Contes du Temps passé* (1697), Bluebeard was a murderous tyrant. In Perrault's tale, Bluebeard entrusts the key to his castle to his new wife, forbidding her to enter one of the rooms. But left on her own, she unlocks the door to find it full of the dead bodies of his former wives.

Behind the scenes

In his own private territory the Commander appears to be almost benign, with an attractive sheepish smile. He treats Offred in a genially patronising way and gradually becomes quite fond of her: 'In fact he is positively daddyish' (p. 193). He seems to have the ability to compartmentalise his life (in a way that Offred cannot manage) so that he can separate her official role as sexual slave from her unofficial role as his companion. In many ways the Commander's motives and needs remain obscure to Offred. They do manage to develop an amiable relationship, which from one point of view is bizarre and from another is entirely ordinary, even boring: 'The fact is that I'm his mistress' (p. 172).

Sexual power politics

The relationship between the Commander and Offred is a game of sexual power politics in which the Commander holds most of the cards, as Offred never allows herself to forget. For all his benign behaviour, he remains trapped in his belief in traditional patriarchy – where the male has primary power over the woman. He believes that this is 'Nature's norm' (p. 232) and that it allows exploitation of women, as his comments and conduct at Jezebel's suggest. Their private sexual encounter there ends in 'futility and **bathos**' (p. 267) and is strongly contrasted with Offred's meeting with Nick later that same evening.

Study focus: 'Walking into the past'

Atwood explores the way memory can obscure history, changing it to fit our own fictional view of the past. The Commander is convinced their outing to Jezebel's is 'like walking into the past' (p. 247) and this delights him. But his memory differs from Offred's version: 'somehow the mix is different'. The Commander yearned for a relationship in the way that Gilead now forbids. All he achieves is 'cheap sex' in a hotel bedroom, and this reduces him from a (moral) figure of higher authority to (immoral) dirty old man. Offred observes that he is diminished: he 'looks smaller, older, like something being dried' (p. 267).

As she leaves his house for the last time, Offred sees the Commander standing at the living-room door, looking old, worried and helpless. Possibly he is expecting his own downfall, for nobody is invulnerable in Gilead. Offred has her revenge, for the balance of power between them has shifted: 'Possibly he will be a security risk, now. I am above him, looking down; he is shrinking' (p. 306).

A secret history

The academics in the 'Historical Notes' section go to some trouble to establish the Commander's identity: he may have been 'Frederick R. Waterford' or 'B. Frederick Judd' (p. 319). Waterford, it is revealed, had a background in market research (which seems most likely), while the more sinister Judd was a military strategist who worked for the CIA. Both of them 'met their ends, probably soon after the events our author describes' (pp. 321–2). Gilead, like Orwell's Oceania, was in the habit of shredding documents in order to revise the official version of state history.

KEY INTERPRETATION A05

The few male characters in this novel seem little more than embodiments of their functions or duties under the patriarchal Gileadean regime – or they are functional in terms of the plot. Most of them have no names but only group identities like 'Angels' or 'Eyes' or 'the doctor', while Professor Pieixoto is a **satirical** sketch of a male academic. Only three male characters are given any identifying characteristics. They are Offred's Commander, her lover Nick and her vanished husband Luke.

KEY QUOTATION A01

The supreme irony of the Commander lies in his yearning for what was before, while justifying the treatment of women under the totalitarian regime. This is realised in the **grotesque tableau** of the brothel. Look closely at the descriptions of the women in Jezebel's. The pathetic jumble of outfits resembles a repugnant meat market; flesh for sale. The Commander says, 'We've given them more than we've taken away' (p. 231). Gilead has replaced the 'desperate' state of women with 'support'. What is missing is 'love'.

Nick

Who is Nick?

- Nick is the Commander's chauffeur, and the Commander's Wife's gardener.
- It is suggested that he may be a member of the resistance group, Mayday.
- Nick's importance lies in his function as Offred's romantic lover.

A mysterious dark stranger

Nick is presented as the central figure of Offred's romantic fantasy, for he is the mysterious dark stranger who is her rescuer through love. He also has a place in her real world, as the Commander's chauffeur and the Commander's Wife's gardener. He 'has a French face, lean, whimsical, all planes and angles, with creases around the mouth where he smiles' (p. 28) and a general air of irreverence, wearing his cap at a jaunty angle, whistling while he polishes the car, and winking at Offred the first day he sees her. At the household prayers he presses his foot against hers, and she feels a surge of sensual warmth which she dare not acknowledge.

In the daytime he is rather a comic figure but at night he is transformed into Offred's romantic lover, the embodiment of sexual desire. This transformation is made all the more poignant because he is always acting under orders, either as the Commander's messenger or as the lover chosen for Offred by the Commander's Wife.

A passive subordinate

As a subordinate, Nick, like Offred, has to remain passive until ordered by the Commander's Wife to go to bed with Offred. On that occasion his attitude is not directly described but veiled by Offred's three different versions of that meeting. Certainly she falls in love with him, and in defiance of danger she returns many times to his room across the dark lawn on her own. Towards the end, she tells him that she is pregnant. Nevertheless, her description of their lovemaking is suggestive rather than explicitly erotic, and Nick tends to remain a mysterious figure.

A lightly sketched character

As a character Nick is very lightly sketched and it is his function as romantic lover which is most significant. We want to believe that he was in love with Offred, and we must assume from the 'Historical Notes' that he did rescue her and that he was a member of the Mayday resistance. Ever elusive, he is the only member of the household not there to see her depart. Even at the end when he appears with the Eyes to take her away, Offred really knows so little about him that she almost accuses him of having betrayed her, until he calls her by her real name and begs her to trust him.

Nick is more important for his role than as a rounded character; he represents romance rather than realism. Their relationship is significant for underlining Offred's powerful conflict of loyalties and the strength of her sexual desire. In the end this becomes more important than her loyalty to Luke, and even her desire to escape.

A02 PROGRESS BOOSTER

It is important to consider the role of Offred's relationship with Nick in terms of creating mounting fear and tension. Offred's account of her dangerous, secret meetings with him is positioned immediately before the violent and brutal Salvagings, at which women who have committed 'unchastity' (p. 287) or adultery are hanged. The tension rises as we are reminded of the increasing peril of her situation.

A01 KEY QUOTATION

We can think of Nick's character as a mirror in which we watch Offred's image begin to change. His relationship with Offred is, like the other characters, played from her first-person perspective and it is a marker of her own progress of sorts. The **narrative** reveals her move away from the pain of her remembered past into a new present which is dominated by the presence of her lover: 'The fact is that I no longer want to leave' (p. 283).

Luke

Who is Luke?

- Luke is Offred's husband.
- He tried to help his family escape across the border.
- Luke's story is told through Offred's ongoing anxiety about his fate.

A Missing Person

Luke, Offred's husband, is one of the Missing Persons in this novel. Probably dead before the **narrative** begins, his memory haunts Offred, fading as her love affair with Nick develops. He is the one person Offred leaves out when she tells the story of her past life to Nick (Chapter 41), though she is still worrying about him at the end (Chapter 44).

A fragmented character

Luke is the most fragmented character in the text, appearing briefly as a name in Chapter 2, and then gradually taking on an identity as Offred's lover, husband and the father of her child. He is a figure whose life story stopped for Offred at a traumatic point in the past: 'Stopped dead in time, in mid-air, among the trees back there, in the act of falling' (p. 239).

Progress booster: Narrative strands

Notice how the fragmented telling of Luke's story, with the painful, awful possibilities of his fate, is woven into Offred's account of the violent coup and its aftermath of security passes, roadblocks and withdrawal of jobs/money for women. We therefore experience the impact of Gilead in several ways – in terms of the internal, or personal, and the external. Luke's story highlights the emotional impact of the takeover, and the two strands of narrative underline for us the chilling possibility of a Gileadean state in our own reality.

Luke as a liberated man

Through Offred's reconstruction Luke appears as a late twentieth-century 'liberated man'. He is full of courage and humour, and is remembered by Offred entirely in his domestic relations with her. He is an older man who has been married before, so that there is an **ironic** parallel drawn between him and the Commander. Offred remembers their affair when she goes with the Commander to Jezebel's, for it is the hotel where she and Luke used to go (Chapter 37).

Luke figures insistently in Offred's recurring nightmare of their failed escape attempt. In the final image he is lying shot, face down in the snow. Offred also recalls his careful preparations and his coolly courageous attempt to take his family to freedom over the Canadian border. His afterlife in the novel is very much the result of Offred's anxieties about what might have happened to him. Is he dead, or in prison? Did he escape? Will he send her a message and help her to escape back into their old family life? 'It's this message, which may never arrive, that keeps me alive. I believe in the message' (p. 116). It is also her hope for this message that keeps the image of Luke alive. The anxieties we may feel for his fate are projections of Offred's own.

KEY INTERPRETATION **A05**

The foundations of Gileadean society appear to be built on gender imbalance, where males hold the power. Yet Atwood commented in 2001: 'Some people think that the society in *The Handmaid's Tale* is one in which all men have power, and all women don't. That is not true.' In what ways might women's power be manifested in the novel?

KEY QUOTATION **A01**

Offred says 'I can't bear to imagine him', of Luke – and yet she does, in painful, descriptive detail that reveals the awful possibilities of the fate of her husband. Look closely at the language used in each of the versions of Luke's story on page 115. Notice how the use of senses and detail diminishes in the third version where he escapes. Offred adds this last version because she needs to hope – but what do we believe is his real fate?

THEMES

Survival

Staying alive

Offred's first priority is to survive physically in the dangerous political climate of Gilead. Everyone is under constant surveillance at home or on the streets, and death is an everyday possibility. A Handmaid is particularly vulnerable if she fails to produce a baby for the state after being posted to three different Commanders. Offred says, of her own childless situation in this, her final posting: *'Give me children or else I die'* (p. 71). This has only one, unambiguous meaning for a Handmaid in Gilead.

Offred is determined to survive, as we know from the beginning when she arrives at the Commander's house: 'I am alive, I live, I breathe, I put my hand out, unfolded, into the sunlight' (p. 18). She retains this vigorous survival instinct even in the most threatening circumstances. In fact she is shocked to find her body still almost independently asserting its demands even after the horrible Particicution ceremony. Sickened by what she has witnessed, she still wants to eat: 'Maybe it's because I've been emptied; or maybe it's the body's way of seeing to it that I remain alive, continue to report its bedrock prayer: *I am, I am. I am, still'* (p. 293). Only near the end does she almost give in to despair. Even then she does not wish to die but to 'keep on living, in any form' (p. 298).

Storytelling as a survival strategy

Offred's second priority is how to survive psychologically and emotionally after the trauma of separation from her husband and child. She has also endured her period of indoctrination at the Rachel and Leah Centre. In her determination to resist Gilead's efforts to erase her individual identity and in order to retain her sanity, she tells herself stories.

Offred uses remembered stories to remind herself of who she was in 'the time before', recognising where she is now, and hoping against hope for the future. Her storytelling becomes her own survival strategy. Her memories are narrated as fragments of stories from the past, interwoven with her record of what is happening to her in the present. Her primary focus now is her physical environment. This is her account of the daily facts of her slavery, and more intimately her own bodily experiences. In contrast to her remembered stories, she copes with her new present by becoming impersonal: 'One detaches oneself. One describes' (p. 106).

A05 **KEY INTERPRETATION**

The theme of survival – for an individual, for a nation, and collectively for the human species – has always been one of Atwood's central concerns. In 1972 she wrote a book called *Survival: A Thematic Guide to Canadian Literature*, where she outlined several meanings of the word 'survival'. The main meaning was 'staying alive', and also that 'the survivor has little after this ordeal that he did not have before, except gratitude for having escaped with his life' (p. 33).

Study focus: Survival through love

The story of Offred's emotional survival is told most fully through her love affair with Nick. It is with him that she rediscovers her self. When she is with Nick, her body and her desires resist the Gileadean authority and he pays attention 'only to the possibilities of my body' (p. 282). Being in love has been edited out by the new regime – but consider how their romance challenges the limits of Gilead's control of the life stories of its citizens.

However, it can be argued that in meeting Nick, Offred survives through luck, and nothing more. Other women in the novel are less fortunate: Moira's brave stand against the regime ends in an inevitable death in the Colonies. Offred's mother suffers the same fate. Ofglen hangs herself. Even the power-sharers, the men, are not immune, for the Commander is vulnerable and finishes as a 'security risk' (p. 306). The staged Prayvaganzas and Particicution ceremonies the women are made to attend function as dramatic tableaux: they are visual representations of the cruel brutality that lies at the heart of a regime where there is no life or love, just a struggle to endure.

Revision task 9: Offred's life in Gilead

Make notes on Offred's life in Gilead. Refer to the ways in which she strives for survival, both physically and psychologically.

Key quotation: 'I don't want to be a doll hung up on the Wall'

The novel examines the effect of totalitarian rule on the individual. Gilead imposes overt control mechanisms such as men in power and strict gender roles. But there is also covert control in the form of fear of betrayal – there is no one Offred can trust. This creates a climate of danger that reduces her to grovelling compliance. Offred's fear climaxes in complete capitulation: 'Everything they taught me at the Red Centre, everything I've resisted, comes flooding in … I don't want to be a doll hung up on the Wall' (p. 298). In the end, what strength does Offred have, beyond her survival instinct?

KEY CONNECTION A04

On page 94 Offred says, 'My name isn't Offred, I have another name'. We cannot be sure of Offred's identity, but it is clear from her **narrative** that that the story is focused on the story of one woman – it is *The* Handmaid's Tale. Offred's real name is very important to her and she does not reveal it to the reader. The Gilead label 'Of-fred' assigned to her indicates that she is owned by a man, a fact that she resists in her inner dialogue.

Identity and the individual

A systematic stripping away of the self

The novel examines our sense of self, or identity, and the challenges that can be brought to bear on the self by the state. The Gileadean state dictates the systematic stripping of identity from women – under its strict rule, women's names are removed and they are reduced instead to gender roles: Handmaid, Econowife, and so on. Those who identify as feminist or are found to be infertile are reduced even further to the sub-human status of Unwoman.

Concealed thoughts and emotions

Offred's account of her present existence often skims the surface of feeling. The opaque descriptions of the house she inhabits are devoid of emotion: 'Mutely the varied surfaces present themselves' (p. 89). But in the sections entitled 'Night', where she tells us that 'The night is mine' (p. 47), she explores her inner identity in personal memory.

Her deprived and limited existence seems to have erased her identity so completely that even in private dialogue with herself, Offred's emotions resist capture. Where do we find them? Her most private thoughts and feelings are concealed from us; they lie in the gaps between the text, in the literal white space on the page:

'Why fight?

That will never do' (p. 237).

Offred's raw core of self exists in the unwritten word – she is not allowed to write. But we can read her grief and pain into these spaces; they make up the core of extreme emotion which threatens to make her lose all hope yet drives her to go on living. Here she is not Offred, but an individual human being with a past and a present self.

Progress booster: 'one and one and one'

The totalitarian state has erased women's identities so efficiently and completely that the Commander is able to say jokingly about women: 'For them, one and one and one and one don't make four' (p. 195). His simple equation evokes a chilling response: in Gilead, for women, the numbers do not make four, or even, as Offred anticipates, 'five or three'. They add up to 'Just one and one and one and one'. Women exist as a 'disconnect'; they are not allowed to complete. Consider the different elements of Offred's life that now exist only as disconnects, or fragments.

Men's identities also erased

It is not only the identity of women that the Gileadean state strips away: men, too, are reduced and objectified, as is evident in the bodies of victims that Offred and Ofglen see hanging on the Wall. The heads of these men are covered to hide their identity, and Offred says, 'Their heads are zeros' (p. 42). She compares them to dolls, scarecrows and stuffed sacks – imagery that disturbs. Offred sees that blood has seeped through the white cloth on one of these faceless, hanging shapes, to form 'another mouth, a small red one' (p. 42); 'a smile of blood'. In this moment of bizarre irony we are reminded of the red, lipsticked mouth of a woman, but these are – were – men.

The hanging is the ultimate reduction of person to inanimate object. Yet Offred resists, refusing to deny these men their identity. She begins to replace their selves: 'You can see the outlines of the features under the white cloth' (p. 42). Others, too, have the right to be seen as an individual.

Uniform

The Republic of Gilead tries to erase identity in other ways. The rigid hierarchy eliminates the individual – all are in uniform, colour-coded to indicate their status or role. Offred and Ofglen are indistinguishable in their Handmaid clothing, just as the Commander wears black. Nick's only claim to an identity beyond his role as chauffeur and gardener is the way he wears his hat to one side. The white wings of Offred's outfit keep her face hidden; her red clothing, a 'red shroud' (p. 31), covers her body completely. Her only means of communicating herself as an individual is with her eyes, as when she meets a Guardian: 'he sees my eyes and I see his, and he blushes' (p. 31). Ironically, the sinister spies of the regime are known as 'Eyes'.

A01 PROGRESS BOOSTER

Large control systems such as governments or prisons seek to institutionalise – a process of capitulation, or loss, of the individual; the institutionalised subject conforms. Notice how characters in *The Handmaid's Tale* who refuse to capitulate may suddenly come into full focus, such as Ofglen on page 176: 'Her face is oval, pink, plump but not fat, her eyes roundish.' Contrast this with Janine, who is fully institutionalised; on the Birth Day she remains indeterminate, reduced to the level of an animal as she 'breathes in and out. Caresses her swollen breasts. Thinks of nothing' (p. 125). Moira and Offred's mother are also vividly depicted, while institutionalised groups such as Commanders' Wives remain amorphous.

Study focus: The dead daffodil

A03

Offred creeps downstairs in darkness to steal a dead daffodil. This small gesture of defiance allows her to remind herself 'of what I once could do' (p. 108). She is intent on pressing the flower and leaving it for whoever comes after her, just as the previous occupant of her room left her scratched words in the closet. These are the ways in which the women of Gilead rediscover precious fragments of identity in the 'tiny peepholes' of possibility (p. 31) that exist in the oppressive regime. For Atwood, being recognised as an individual, a fully acknowledged self, is vital; she has aptly summed this up in her poem 'This is a photograph of me' (published in her first poetry collection, *The Circle Game*, 1998), where she at first appears to be describing a landscape, but then tells us that, if we look closely enough, we will be able to see her.

Power politics

State tyranny

The novel challenges state tyranny and social engineering, which rules out choice, emotion or free will for most men as well as women. Its concerns include gender politics and basic human rights. It can therefore be seen as being about more than just a feminist dystopia.

The Republic of Gilead is a 'grand **narrative**' – it would describe itself as heroic. It would explain its own history in terms of its ideals, which are comprehensive, unchallenged and male-centred. Offred, as a woman and a Handmaid, is marginalised in the new regime. But her tale – her own 'little narrative' – refuses to accept the Gileadean state's idea of itself as heroic.

An alternative, feminised version of history

Offred's main interest is not political – she does not concern herself with state power politics. She is not even really interested in Ofglen's Mayday resistance movement. But her story is a challenge to the absolute authority of Gilead. She gives us an alternative, feminised version of history.

In her 1981 Amnesty International address, when she was already thinking about *The Handmaid's Tale*, Atwood said, about writers: 'The writer retains three attributes that power-mad regimes cannot tolerate: a human imagination, in the many forms it may take; the power to communicate; and hope' (*Second Words*, p. 397). Offred shows her defiance of Gilead in her inner freedom: her imagination, her desires and her own spark of hope. These are things that the state cannot stamp out. As Offred, female storyteller, says: 'there will be an ending, to the story, and real life will come after it' (p. 49).

A failed utopia

As the narrative demonstrates, Gilead is a failed utopia for everyone. Everything is in short supply – evident in the rationed foodstuffs and goods, and the lack of sexual choice for both women and men. Most important is the sharp decline in the birth rate and reproduction; women are reduced to their biological function as child-bearers and denied any sexual freedom at all at any age.

In Gilead, the crisis in reproduction has affected men's lifestyles too. Any male practice which inhibits reproduction is severely punished, so that male doctors who formerly practised abortion, or homosexuals, or Roman Catholic priests (as well as nuns) who took vows of chastity are all executed and their bodies hung on the Wall. Pornography, sexual violence and infidelity are all outlawed, but so is falling in love.

Key quotation: Atwood's use of imagery **A02**

Offred says, 'The air got too full, once, of chemicals, rays, radiation, the water swarmed with toxic molecules'. Look closely at the language throughout this section on page 122. Examine Atwood's use of imagery, listing and use of the pronoun 'you' – we might consider the text here to be speaking out, addressing the reader. Look also at her **grotesque** images for an 'Unbaby', a disfigured child that might be born with 'a snout like a dog's', or 'webbed hands and feet'. What do you think Atwood is suggesting here?

Progress booster: The Gilead of the future? **A02**

On page 187 Offred says, 'All they needed to do is push a few buttons'. As readers, we may find the concept of the Gileadean state all the more sinister because of its awful potential for existence in our own near future. Offred's narrative constantly reminds us of different aspects of our contemporary society. Her previous life, with its plastic cards, 'Compubank' and 'Compucount', is chillingly familiar: we now think nothing of computer storage of our personal information. Our technological society is under scrutiny in the novel – what do you think it has to say about our easy acceptance of such things?

Imprisonment and imagination

The present as a trap

Offred exists in a time trap of the present, where she feels she is living with her face pressed up against a wall. Only in memory and imagination does she have any freedom of choice, and it is through her storytelling that she invents a life which has more to it than the numb, limited space of her reality: 'What I need is perspective. The illusion of depth … Otherwise you live in the moment. Which is not where I want to be' (p. 153).

Study focus: Double vision **A02**

Make sure you can explore how Offred's **narrative** is full of her double vision, where she sees the present through her memories of her past. She lives in a familiar place which, after the revolution, is no longer familiar. But everywhere she walks in the prison that this, her home town of Cambridge, Massachusetts, has become, she is led straight into the free landscape of memory: 'To the right, if you could walk along, there's a street that would take you down towards the river. There's a boathouse where they kept the sculls once, and some bridges' (p. 40). Look for other moments where the narrative is 'doubled' in this way, such as the opening to the novel, where her memories of a previous freedom collide with her new, restricted present.

A05 KEY INTERPRETATION

In *The Cambridge Introduction to Margaret Atwood*, H. S. Macpherson says: 'Atwood has always used punctuation in her own unique way, and in this novel, her style reflects the loose connections between fantasy and reality'. Offred's narrative uses commas in an unconventional way, when moving from her prison of the present moment into the freedom of memory: 'We wait, the clock in the hall ticks, Serena lights another cigarette, I get into the car. It's a Saturday morning, it's a September, we still have a car' (p. 94).

Memory stories

In a curious way the plot mirrors Offred's memory stories, as characters from her remembered past reappear. Moira is there in Gilead in the flesh twice, while Offred's mother's ghost is resurrected twice (on films which Moira tells Offred she sees at the Rachel and Leah Centre in Chapters 7 and 39). Offred's daughter is brought back in a photograph which Serena Joy shows to her (Chapter 35). Of course these presences do not remain with Offred; her story is an emotive mix of moments of joy, but also stabs of pain at their loss and her recognition of her own powerlessness. Her storytelling cannot change her entrapment in Gilead but it does give her the power to escape into imagination. It becomes an act of psychological survival.

Escape into memory

Some of Offred's memories may be nostalgic – but they are also her chief escape. Alone in her room in the darkness, she says, 'the night is my time out. Where should I go?' (p. 47). When her world closes around her like the suffocating walls of a cell, she selects from her memory bank which story she will tell about absent presences, like her dearest friend Moira, her mother, her little daughter, her husband Luke. So, while these may be stories of loss and mourning, they are also part of her imaginative life and freedom – and they keep these ghosts from the past with her. She says, when remembering Moira, 'I've tried to make it sound as much like her as I can. It's a way of keeping her alive' (p. 256).

Many of Offred's memory stories are also triggered by association with places or events in the present. As she says, 'You'll have to forgive me. I'm a refugee from the past, and like other refugees I go over the customs and habits of being I've left or been forced to leave behind me' (p. 239). Her narrative shows the complex ways that memory works, where thoughts in the present moment contain traces of other times and events.

The language of the body

She may be cocooned in the uniform that defines her role as Handmaid, but underneath her layers, Offred's body is her own space. She resists the way Gilead reduces her physically to a breeder. She tells the story of her sensations, emotions and desires. She has the power to tell a different story from the one already scripted for her: in the language she uses to describe her own physiology, Offred finds freedom. She talks about her body as a wilderness. Her womb is a dark, cosmic space with the moon gliding across it every month. Her laughter, which wells up from her body, is volcanic.

KEY INTERPRETATION A05

Feminist critic Hélène Cixous wrote in *The Laugh of the Medusa*, 1975: 'I, too, have felt so full of luminous torrents that I could burst.' Cixous challenges male patriarchy with her definition of '*jouissance*' – the idea that women should be celebrated in terms of excess, rather than lack.

Key quotation: Reclaiming the body   A01

Offred describes her body as 'my own territory' … 'where only I know the footing' (p. 83). Her body is imprisoned inside her Handmaid's outfit; the red clothing covers her completely, and the white wings around her head limit her ability to see. Her view of the world is restricted and she must look through 'tunnels of cloth' (p. 29). Notice how, although she is subjected to the clinical copulation ceremony each month, she still sees her body as her own space. It may be violated by the Ceremony, but she insists on reclaiming it.

PROGRESS CHECK

Section One: Check your understanding

These tasks will help you to evaluate your knowledge and skills level in this particular area.

1. What is the significance of Offred's relationship with Nick? Write a paragraph explaining your view.

2. Make notes on the role of the Aunts in Gilead, and the two contexts in which we see Aunt Lydia – what is our opinion of her character?

3. List three ways in which the Republic of Gilead erases Offred's identity as a woman.

4. Identify three things Offred does which demonstrate her subversive resistance to the regime.

5. What is the significance of Offred's remembered stories? Write a short paragraph explaining your ideas.

6. 'The failed dystopia of Gilead can be considered a warning to twentieth century society.' List two issues in contemporary society that come under scrutiny in the novel, and write a short paragraph on each.

7. Find three instances in the novel where we can see Offred's mother as a heroic figure.

8. Identify three statements or events within Offred's narrative that show how much she is stimulated by her meetings with the Commander in his study.

9. What is the significance of the men's bodies that hang on the Wall in Chapter 6? Write a paragraph explaining your view.

10. Make a table listing four or five things we learn from Offred's narrative about Serena Joy's character.

Section Two: Working towards the exam

Choose one of the following three tasks, which require longer, more developed answers:

1. 'Offred's only freedom in Gilead is that which her imagination provides.' Do you agree?

2. 'Gilead is a state where men hold all the power and women have none.' To what extent do you agree with this statement?

3. Compare the characters of Offred, Moira and Ofglen. What models of heroism do they provide?

A01 PROGRESS BOOSTER

For each Section Two task, read the question carefully, select the key areas you need to address, and plan an essay of six to seven points. Write a first draft, giving yourself an hour to do so. Make sure you include supporting evidence for each point, including quotations.

Progress check (rate your understanding on a level of 1 – low, to 5 – high)	1	2	3	4	5
The key actions, motives and thoughts of major and minor characters in the text					
The different ways you can interpret particular characters' words and actions					
How characterisation is linked to key themes and ideas					
The significance of key themes and ideas within the text					
How some key themes (such as survival and imprisonment) are linked to context					

GENRE

Defining genre

How do we define a **genre** at the present time? Utopias and dystopias are evidently two sides of the same coin, and it is worth thinking about the genre or literary form to which they both belong. Today we think of genre not as a rigid classification system but rather as a set of conventions or codes or 'family resemblances' (in plot or form or kind of language used). Our expectations of genre are formed from all the other texts we have read, as we look for familiar signs that tell us whether to expect a detective novel or a romance, for example.

These genre conventions influence the choices writers make, just as they structure our expectations as readers. When they write, all authors are responding in some way to the society to which they belong, and **postmodern** critics have encouraged us to see genres as socially constructed in this way.

Utopia and dystopia

Utopias and anti-utopias are not merely fantasy worlds. As Krishan Kumar describes in his book *Utopianism* (1991), they are imaginary places 'that nevertheless exist tantalisingly (or frighteningly) on the edge of possibility, somewhere just beyond the boundary of the real' (p. 1). These fictions always have a kind of mirror relationship to the writer's own world. They may offer models for the future, or more frequently they may make **satiric** attacks on present society.

As political or social commentary, utopian fictions have a strongly **didactic** element – they aim to teach moral values. Margaret Atwood said in a review of Marge Piercy's *Woman on the Edge of Time* (1976), 'Utopias are products of the moral rather than the literary sense.' They may deliver strong warnings against the consequences of particular kinds of political and social behaviour.

Study focus: The importance of historical context

A03

Bear in mind that utopias and dystopias need to be read with some knowledge of the context of their own time; the reader needs to understand some of the issues which dominated the society in which they were produced. Sir Thomas More's *Utopia* (1516) is concerned with the possibilities for a better society that were being opened up by the discovery of the New World of America. Nearly 500 years later, *The Handmaid's Tale* also explores the possibilities in a potential future, warning against threats of environmental pollution, religious fundamentalism and state surveillance that may exist in contemporary society.

KEY CONTEXT **A03**

Writers have always invented imaginary good societies (utopias) and imaginary bad societies (anti-utopias or **dystopias**) in order to comment on distinctive features and trends of their own societies. In fact, the tradition of utopian fiction in Western culture goes back to the Ancient Greeks with Plato's *Republic*, written about 350BC.

KEY CONTEXT **A03**

Atwood is very aware of the power of shared understanding of genre conventions, and in an interview shortly after the publication of *The Handmaid's Tale* she commented: 'You have to understand what the [literary] form is doing, how it works, before you say, "Now we're going to make it different, we're going to do this thing which is unusual, we're going to turn it upside down, we're going to move it so it includes something which isn't supposed to be there, we're going to surprise the reader"' (*Conversations*, p. 193).

The Handmaid's Tale as feminine dystopia

Atwood made crucial changes to the dystopian genre with *The Handmaid's Tale*, for as she has pointed out, utopias and dystopias are traditionally seen as masculine in genre terms. She feminised the dystopia by making her storyteller a woman. When in 1998 she gave a series of talks to students in France about the writing of *The Handmaid's Tale*, she spoke of her extensive reading of utopias and dystopias; most of her examples were written by men.

Systems of social control

Atwood emphasised that the meeting point between utopias and dystopias was that they were both representations of arranged societies. These were characterised by highly regulated systems of social control and punishment for those who violated the laws of that society. She commented: 'Both utopias and dystopias have the habit of cutting off the hands and feet and even heads of those who don't fit in the scheme' (Interview in *Lire Margaret Atwood: The Handmaid's Tale*, p. 20).

Interestingly, a utopia can quickly change into its opposite, depending on the point of view of the narrator and whether or not he or she benefits from the new social order. As the Commander counters Offred's objections to Gilead: 'Better never means better for everyone … It always means worse, for some' (p. 222).

The features of a dystopia

The main features of a dystopia are patriarchal rule, totalitarianism and dictatorship (as opposed to a consensus of opinion on the laws found in utopias, according to Atwood). Other characteristics are strict social hierarchies, and the erasure of individual difference in the interests of a 'collective good'. A dystopian society will use censorship, **propaganda** and state control of the language used by its citizens. We might compare Gilead's invented biblical **rhetoric** and its new vocabulary for Handmaids' greetings and collective rituals with Orwell's Newspeak in *Nineteen Eighty-Four*. In both cases language is changed into an instrument not for communication purposes but to smother dissenting voices, particularly those of women.

Political and social protest writing

Related to utopian or dystopian fiction is the genre of political and social protest writing. This type of writing comments on aspects of society and has at its core issues of power and powerlessness. Its main concern lies in its protest, and central themes of this genre are oppression and domination. We might think of political and social protest fiction in terms of the power struggles it portrays.

Political and social protest fiction may present us with models of rebellion, corruption and control. This kind of writing may scrutinise how we organise ourselves as humans, in our internal, domestic settings of home, or in the larger, external arenas of government. It may also examine power in the way that society uses language. We can explore elements of this genre in *The Handmaid's Tale*: in its imagined setting, the novel examines roles in society – those who wield power and those who have none, and how they behave. See **Part Five: Contexts and interpretations** for a discussion of other works in this genre.

AO4 KEY CONNECTION

In her talks to students in 1998, Atwood offered a much shorter list of utopian fictions by women that included Charlotte Perkins Gilman's *Herland* (1915) and Marge Piercy's *Woman on the Edge of Time*. She mentioned only one feminist dystopia, *The Stepford Wives*, which was made into a film in 1974 from a novel written by a man, Ira Levin.

The **narrative** structure of *The Handmaid's Tale* is fragmented: it echoes the sense of shock and disorientation Offred experiences. It is a broken narrative – arranged in disjointed, fragmented sections where memory blurs with reality. The story shifts abruptly from one scene to another and from the present to the past, so that Offred's present situation and her past history are only gradually revealed.

STRUCTURE

External and internal story

There are a number of ways to explore structure in the novel – in fact we could argue that the text refuses to be limited by definition, or labelling, in the same way as Offred herself.

Broadly speaking, the text is organised into what we might think of as external and internal sections. Externally, Offred recounts the everyday monotony and bleak existence now imposed on her. In these sections, what we understand as our ordinary experience of living – shopping, a waiting room, at home, a birthday – becomes something much more disturbing. Other external events constructed by Gilead, such as the Prayvaganzas, take on the nightmarish qualities of a frightening **dystopian** world. In the 'Night', or internal, sections, alone in her room, Offred reveals more of her inner thoughts and emotions to us. Throughout, she acts as our guide and we share in her difficult process of trying to adjust to the new regime.

The 'Night' sections: flashback

Reading the novel is an exercise of reconstruction as we piece together present details with fragments of remembered experience, revealed by **flashbacks**. At the beginning there are few flashbacks, for we, like Offred, are trapped in the present time. The first flashback occurs in Chapter 3, and there are brief references to Luke in Chapters 2 and 5.

It is in the 'Night' sections that the flashback technique is most obvious and most sustained, for this is Offred's 'time out' when she is free to revisit her remembered past. It is here that we gain a sense of Offred as a presence in the novel, with a history – at these times her narrative offers us a patchwork of glimpses of her previous life with her husband and daughter.

Study focus: The Commander's study

We can view the sections where Offred visits the Commander in his study as moments in which the freedom of Offred's past collides with her present imprisonment. Offred and the Commander play Scrabble, a game now historical (and forbidden). In their games, they reconstruct bogus **neologisms**: they 'make words with them that don't exist, words like smurt and crup, giggling over them' (p. 220). Ironically, it is only under the Commander's terms of her present imprisonment that Offred is permitted to become something more like the free-thinking woman of her past. Look closely at these sections: do her visits to the Commander create freedom for Offred, or emphasise her lack of it?

A present constructed from the past

The way the narrative is structured, to shift between the present and her remembered past, means that we view Offred's story through the lens of her own history. As the story unfolds, the growing knowledge of Offred's lost life and loved ones increases our sense of despair for her. Historians may claim that we understand our selves by drawing on our knowledge of the past, and this focus on history is echoed in the Gileadean state. Offred's narrative is framed by historical scripture, and the **oxymoronic** 'Historical Notes' from a future in which the Republic of Gilead has been swept aside. Those in the future must reach into the past to discover her story. We understand, finally, that by the time we read Offred's story she no longer exists.

LANGUAGE

Storytelling as an act of resistance

The Handmaid's Tale is a woman's autobiographical **narrative** that challenges the absolute authority of Gilead. It highlights the importance of storytelling as an act of resistance against oppression; the story becomes a kind of individual political statement. We might approach Offred's narrative through Atwood's own comments as a writer who is an active member of Amnesty International:

> 'I'm an artist … and in any monolithic [large and powerful] regime I would be shot. They always do that to artists. Why? Because the artists are messy. They don't fit. They make squawking noises. They protest.' (*Conversations*, p. 183)

Offred, as teller of this tale, insists on voicing her own point of view when the regime demands total silence. But her freedom is so limited that she cannot tell her story while the Gileadean state exists. She can only tell it after she has escaped. We learn at the end that Offred's narrative is a transcript of recordings that have been found on an archaeological site. What we have is a later reconstruction of Offred's own account, which she gave after escaping to freedom. Her words form a historical artefact, and we understand her story to be a voice of protest against oppression.

Prison or survival narrative?

We can analyse narrative technique in the novel by thinking of Offred's story as a woman's prison narrative. Just as Offred herself is enclosed by her Handmaid's costume and entrapped in the domestic spaces of the Commander's house, so her story is enclosed by the quotations from scripture which begin the novel and the 'Historical Notes' at the end. Offred understands how tyrannical the rulers of Gilead are. In recording her words, she has shown her determination to outlast the brutal regime and make her protest heard. Her story might therefore be seen as a woman's survival narrative. One of her major survival strategies is her secret storytelling, for she is the voice of the excluded other within Gilead.

Study focus: Offred's affair with Nick

Crucial for Offred is her love affair with Nick (Chapters 40 and 41), which has all the conventional features of a romantic love story and possibly even a happy ending. Yet in the circumstances it is the most unlikely plot that could have been devised, and Offred tells it with a kind of dazzled disbelief in its reality. Her relationship with Nick is part of her survival story and it is interesting that her supposed escape comes from this illicit, romantic affair. Look carefully at where these sections sit within the framework of the narrative, so that you have a clear picture of how the relationship develops.

Public and private lives

Offred's story as a record of daily life is presented with scrupulous attention to realistic detail. She records the unexciting monotony of her daily life as a Handmaid, as well as its crises, both public and personal. There are the public meetings like the Birth Day, the Prayvaganza and the terrible Salvaging; there is of course the monthly Ceremony as a semi-public event; there are her own significant private events, like her secret meetings with the Commander and their outing to Jezebel's.

KEY INTERPRETATION **A04**

For a discussion of Offred's narrative voice, see M. Dvorak, 'What's in a Name? Readers as both Pawns and Partners of Margaret Atwood's Strategy of Control', in J. M. Lacroix and J. Leclaire, eds, *Margaret Atwood: The Handmaid's Tale / Le Conte de la servante*, 1998.

Other women's stories

Offred's **narrative** tells the stories of many other women as well as her own. Some of these are fixed in the past and some end even while she is telling her story. Moira's story, like Offred's mother's, is one of female heroism. It extends into the present, for she too becomes an inmate at the Rachel and Leah Centre, and Offred recalls with delight Moira's courage and outrageousness in Chapters 13, 15 and 22. Offred finds Moira again at Jezebel's in Chapter 37, and tells the story of Moira's life as a rebel in Chapter 38. Hers is one of the unfinished stories embedded in this narrative, for Offred never sees Moira again after that night.

Progress booster: Hidden stories   **A01**

There are also shorter story fragments about other Handmaids, all of them rebels or victims or both, which form a sad subtext to Offred's survival narrative. There is the story of Offred's unnamed predecessor at the Commander's house, of whom all she knows is the scribbled secret message (Chapter 9) and scraps of information about how she hanged herself (Chapter 29). Consider: what kind of judgement are these stories intended to pass on the social engineering policies of Gilead?

The motif of doubles

For Offred, the anonymous woman who was in her room before her is her own ghostly **double**: 'How could I have believed I was alone in here? There were always two of us. Get it over, she says' (p. 305). This **motif** of doubles recurs in the story of Ofglen: 'Doubled, I walk the street' (p. 33). Yet Ofglen turns out to be more like Moira's double than Offred's, for she too is a rebel in disguise, a member of the Mayday Resistance movement and a whisperer of irreverent comments at the Prayvaganza. But her story does have an ending, for she commits suicide after the Salvaging (Chapter 44).

Whether women are rebels or willing victims, their chances of survival are slim, as the story of Janine illustrates. She appears and reappears, marking the various stages of a Handmaid's career – from willing victim at the Rachel and Leah Centre where she almost has a nervous breakdown (Chapter 33), to her moment of triumph as the pregnant Ofwarren whose Birth Day is attended by all the Handmaids (Chapters 19 and 21). Her last, frightening, appearance is after the Particicution, where she holds a clump of bloodstained hair (Chapter 43). Janine has lost all hold on reality. She is also one of Offred's doubles, a dreadful warning of what may happen if Offred, too, gives up hope.

Offred also tells the story of the Commander's Wife, with **flashbacks** to her earlier career as a television personality on a gospel show in Chapters 3 and 8. We might say that Offred's account presents Serena Joy as another of her own doubles, trapped like herself by Gileadean **ideology**. In one of her more curious anecdotes, Offred is disguised as Serena Joy when she has to wear her blue cloak to go with the Commander to Jezebel's, and she is forced to look at her own face in Serena Joy's silver mirror to put on her make-up.

Offred insists on telling the stories of other, silenced women. Her words contradict Gilead's claims to absolute mastery and its myth of female submissiveness. We can describe her narrative as **symbolic**: she writes on behalf of all women from the past and from the present who have no rights of representation.

Offred the self-conscious narrator

Another dimension to Offred's complex **narrative** is that of the self-conscious narrator. Offred is continually drawing our attention to her storytelling process, commenting on the way that the act of telling a story shapes and changes real experience, and giving reasons why she needs to tell her story at all (see Chapters 7, 23, 40 and 41). The narrative deliberately draws the reader into the action as it happens by sometimes addressing the reader as '*Dear You*' (p. 49, for example). In this way we are guided into our role as participants and we share in Offred's moral dilemmas.

Offred understands that texts are created by their *readers* as well as by their writers: meanings are not fixed by the narrator but may have different resonances for different readers in the light of their own experiences. She recognises that she does not have ultimate authority over what her story means, and that meanings are always a matter of perspective. In this way we can think of the novel as being **postmodern**. Offred is always questioning herself on how 'true' her story is, or where the boundaries lie between fiction and reality.

Study focus: An unreliable narrator

A02

Offred comments, 'Tell, rather than write, because I have nothing to write with and writing is in any case forbidden' (p. 49). Although we are reading Offred's narrative in written form, it is important remember that it is actually a woman's oral narrative, and this is confirmed at the end in the 'Historical Notes'. Offred also draws our attention to the fact that her telling is a reconstruction after events have happened, and that she is not always a trustworthy narrator. When she is telling us about her first sexual encounter with Nick in Chapter 40, she teases us by giving us several versions, at the end of which she says, 'It didn't happen that way either. I'm not sure how it happened; not exactly' (p. 275). Memory, like language, is not entirely reliable when it comes to reconstructing reality.

The role of storytelling

For Offred storytelling serves many functions: as her main survival technique, it allows her to record her present circumstances in an eyewitness account. It also allows her to escape from the present back into memory. We may even view the narrative as looking to the future, because she is always hoping for the day when she will get out of Gilead and be reunited with Luke and her lost daughter.

Storytelling also becomes a substitute for dialogue with others, as Offred invents her listeners: 'By telling you anything at all, I'm at least believing in you, I believe you're there, I believe you into being' (p. 279). She knows it is the only message she can send to the outside world from her imprisonment and she struggles to tell it, trusting that one day her message will be delivered: 'A story is like a letter. *Dear You*, I'll say. Just *you*, without a name … *You* can mean thousands' (pp. 49–50). Like the Ancient Mariner, Offred's compulsion to tell compels us to listen: 'After all you've been through, you deserve whatever I have left, which is not much but includes the truth' (p. 280).

A04 **KEY CONNECTION**

In Samuel Taylor Coleridge's *Rime of the Ancient Mariner* (1834), the narrator, who alone of all his crew survives terrifying experiences at sea, lives on and is condemned as a penance to 'pass from land to land' retelling his tale with his 'strange power of speech'.

An inner voice rich in imagery

Offred's outer life is very constricted and drained of emotion, but her inner life has an energy and poetic quality which enable her to survive emotionally as well as physically in the **metaphorically** stony soil of Gilead. There is a marked difference between the language Offred uses to record her muted everyday life, and the language of her real life of feeling and memory, which is filled with rich imagery. This shows her entirely different perception of herself and her world from the one imposed by Gilead.

In her Handmaid's role Offred's language of description – of her room, the household, her walks, and the Ceremony – emphasises her isolation. She deliberately filters out emotion for as long as possible, though it seeps in through her imagery. One example of this would be when she likens the blank space on the ceiling where the light fitting has been removed to a 'wreath' (p. 17). Behind the blankness lies Offred's fear of torture, injury and death.

Offred's wordplay

Sometimes Offred's realistic recording is overlaid by memories of the past closely associated with particular places that she passes on her walks, so that the present dissolves into landscapes of memory. Often, however, she defends herself against nostalgia by playing with language, endlessly exploring the potential for multiple meanings in a word. Such wordplay is evidence of Offred's sharpness of mind as well as her moral refusal to flatten out language as happens in Gilead. It is an amusement for her, while it also makes us aware of the value of words, warning us to avoid the linguistic traps that political **rhetoric** may use.

Study focus: Offred's love of language

Offred has a great love for puns, as she delights in the random connections between words that sound the same but have different meanings. For instance, when sitting in a chair alone in her room she thinks about the word 'chair' and how it may refer to 'the leader of a meeting' or 'a mode of execution' (p. 120). Working across language borders, she thinks how the same word has an entirely different meaning in French, where it is the word for 'flesh' (p. 120). Look for other examples of this; just as she refuses to submit to her new name, she refuses to allow language to compartmentalise and define her.

The use of irony

Another of Offred's strategies for mental survival is her use of **irony**. She has a lively sense of the absurd and it would be wrong to forget the comic dimension in this novel. Her simmering humour bubbles up even in the copulation ceremony – 'There's something hilarious about this' (p. 106) – and when she is invited by the Commander to play an illegal game of Scrabble with him it is all she can do not to 'shriek with laughter, fall off my chair' (p. 148).

The Scrabble game is a crucial turning point in their relationship. Offred explodes into muffled laughter when she is back in her room and her language at this point is a disturbing mix of merriment and hysteria tinged with irony. She compares her laughter to an epileptic fit which comes upon her involuntarily, and the images she uses are not simply about loss of control but about splitting, breakage and damage, to the point where she explodes: 'Red all over the cupboard, mirth rhymes with birth' (p. 156). Standing in the cupboard, she is aware of her predecessor's message, and her laughter is tinged with an ironic awareness that she, like the other hanged Handmaid, is trapped: 'There's no way out of here' (p. 156).

Key quotation: Delicious words

A02

Offred's visits to the Commander give her reason to hope, which is cautiously signalled in her last word of this episode – not 'open' (not yet) but 'opening' (p. 156). The Scrabble game appeals to Offred because it gives her an opportunity to play with language, to resurrect obscure words like 'Zygote' (p. 149) and even to make up nonsense words. Her delight is almost physical as she compares the letters in the game to sweets: 'I would like to put them into my mouth … The letter C. Crisp, slightly acid on the tongue, delicious' (p. 149). Her word games are some of the 'tiny peepholes' (p. 31) in the bleak, superficial life imposed upon her. They are a part of her resistance to Gilead's patriarchal regime, which allows her to survive psychologically.

A 'feminine' language

Offred's private **narrative**, which is the secret of her emotional survival, is focused on memory and her own female body. The language of her body – her physical sensations, emotions and desires – uses poetic imagery and imaginary landscapes. In writing about her body Offred shows how a feminine voice can find a way of speaking even when silenced by the male order. Her intimate narrative is as subversive as the flowers in the Commander's Wife's garden: 'Whatever is silenced will clamour to be heard, though silently' (p. 161).

There are a small number of recurring images which form patterns or 'image clusters' throughout the narrative. They refer to the human body (hands, feet, faces, eyes, blood, wombs). Images from nature also run through the text, such as flowers, gardens, changing seasons, colour and light – especially moonlight (see **Extract analyses**, p. 20 and p. 25). Offred's images, all related to nature and organic processes, create a natural, 'feminine', language that works in opposition to Gilead's unnatural, polluted, technological nightmare.

Revision task 11: Offred's capacity for life

A02

'Oh God oh God. How can I keep on living'. (p. 205). How does Offred's narrative voice work to contradict the sense of desolation in her statement? Make notes on how Offred's narrative voice works to contradict the sense of desolation in her statement.

The language of Gilead

The ideas that underpin Gilead's society are based on the Old Testament of the Bible, where in feminist terms the law of God can be interpreted as patriarchal authority. There are far more references to the Old than to the New Testament. In Gilead, the archaic, or old-fashioned, language of patriarchy is used as a mechanism for social control: the biblical patriarch, or 'father of the human race', Jacob, is the state hero. The name Gilead is closely associated with Jacob, for that was the place where, according to the biblical story, he set up his heap of stones as witness to God and established his household, family line, and flocks and herds.

The first quotation in the **epigraph**, from the Old Testament, Genesis 30:1–3, forms the basis of the novel and is repeated many times in the text, most notably in the family Bible reading before the monthly Ceremony. There are echoes of it in the name of the Rachel and Leah Centre and in Offred's remark that *'Give me children, or else I die'* (p. 71) can have more than one meaning for her as a Handmaid. There is one long passage from the New Testament (I Timothy 2:9–15) which is used at the mass marriage ceremony in Chapter 34. This is part of Gilead's **propaganda** about male domination and female submission.

A05 **KEY INTERPRETATION**

Critics have suggested that the words Offred uses in the game may be a code for her hidden protest against the regime's sexual coercion and silencing of women, with 'Larynx', 'Valance', and 'Zygote' (p. 149), followed later by 'Quandary' and 'Rhythm' (p. 164). That may be so, though the protest is a very indirect one, for these words are scattered among others that could not possibly have that significance. Together they make up a list of the most valuable words for winning points in a Scrabble game. It is no wonder that Offred often wins, though out of good manners she sometimes lets the Commander win a game.

A04 **KEY CONNECTION**

The Commandments of the Republic of Gilead are variants of the Ten Commandments in the Bible. Check Exodus 20:1–19 against Gilead's prohibitions to see the ways in which the originals have been manipulated.

KEY CONTEXT **A03**

In addition to Gilead's selective use of biblical language to support and enforce a system of **patriarchy**, there are also other, wider references: Aunt Lydia's words of encouragement to the Handmaids, *'From each ... according to her ability; to each according to his needs'* (p. 127), which she claims is from St Paul, is actually from a description of systems of production by Karl Marx. References to Freud in 'Pen Is Envy' (p. 196) and Milton's sonnet (1673) in 'They also serve ...' (p. 28) also emphasise women's subservience to men.

Gilead's misuse of biblical language

The leaders of Gilead understand very well how, like the army and the police, language can be used as part of state repression and to control. In Gilead, biblical references are part of every level of **discourse**. To use language in this way is to operate by stealth – the names we use in our society shape the way we think about our lives. It is through words that Gilead seeks to control people's minds: Aunt Lydia's slogan 'Gilead is within you' (p. 33) can be seen as blasphemous, being a **parody** of Christ's words 'The Kingdom of God is within you'. It shows the ways Gilead works to embed its ideas in everybody's lives.

This abuse of language, where words are taken from the Bible and used for oppression, is one of the most shocking features of Gilead. The law enforcers are named after Old Testament figures, whether they are 'Guardian Angels' or the 'Eyes of the Lord'. This contributes to the oppressive tone of the novel. (It reminds us of Orwell's 'Newspeak', where the Ministry of Truth should really be named the Ministry of Lies). With its **euphemisms**, **neologisms** and biblical misquotations, language is destabilised, and this in turn leads to the anxieties and uncertainties which are part of Gileadean daily life.

Progress booster: Language and the role of women

Notice how women's domestic roles are given biblical significance, for example the Handmaids, and the female servants who become 'Marthas', (a biblical reference to the woman who served Christ). The 'Econowives' are an exception to this; their name seems more influenced by late twentieth-century advertising than by Scripture.

Gilead's misogyny, or contempt for women, is made plain with 'Jezebel's' as the name of the state-run brothel; this name suggests the scandal of female sexuality. In a country where God is treated as a 'NATIONAL RESOURCE' (p. 225), biblical names filter into the commercial world. The car brand names available are 'Behemoth', 'Whirlwind' or 'Chariot', and shops have been renamed with pictorial signs which reflect biblical texts, such as 'Lilies of the Field' and 'All Flesh'. Such names attach a superficial label of 'holiness' to shopping by coupons in a society in which everything is rationed – an **ironic** comment, perhaps?

KEY CONTEXT **A03**

The Aunts' names may be derived from pre-Gileadean women's products; they suggest cakes and cosmetics, for example, Aunt Elizabeth (Elizabeth Arden cosmetics), Aunt Sara (Sara Lee cakes), Aunt Helena (Helena Rubenstein cosmetics). An alternative explanation is that many of the Aunts' names are biblical: Lydia was a rich woman converted to Christianity by St Paul (Acts 16:14); Elizabeth was the mother of John the Baptist (Luke 1:23–25); Sara was the wife of Abraham who conceived a son in her old age (Genesis 21:1–5).

Words and silence

Gilead uses and abuses the words of the Bible in the same way that it appropriates the slogans of the free society it has overthrown. The Word is in the mouths of men only; the Bible is kept locked up and only Commanders are allowed to read it. Even the hymns are edited, and Moira's rebellious version of '"There is a Balm in Gilead"' (p. 230) is muffled by the massed choir of the Handmaids. Offred prays in her own private way, saying her version of the Lord's Prayer (Chapter 30) or crying out to God in despair (Chapter 45), but here, as elsewhere, her woman's voice is muted.

'Historical Notes': A different perspective

Offred's own words end when she climbs up into the black van, but the novel does not finish there. The 'Historical Notes' which follow function as a supplement to her story. They help us to put one woman's autobiographical record into historical perspective. The 'Notes' introduce another futuristic scenario, which is different from the story of Gilead. They have a different narrator (a male professor) in a different place, at a different time – some two centuries after Offred has told her story.

The setting for the futuristic conference is the University of Denay, Nunavit, in Arctic Canada. Women and Native peoples obviously have some status, for the Chair is a woman professor, Maryann Crescent Moon, and the conference participants go on nature walks and eat fish from the sea, which suggests an unpolluted environment very different from Gilead.

The professor gives a detailed account of how Offred's story was recovered from old cassette tapes made between the 1960s and the 1980s. In this way he establishes a historical context for Offred's **narrative**. However, his jokes about 'tail' and 'Frailroad' (p. 313) suggest that sexist attitudes have not changed very much in 200 years. His narrative demonstrates the same masculinist values as the leaders of the Gilead regime, who had modelled themselves as the Sons of Jacob – patriarchs from the Old Testament.

He is interested in establishing the authenticity of Offred's tale and its value as objective historical evidence, but he sidesteps the critical moral issues raised by her account: 'Our job is not to censure but to understand' (p. 315). He is not concerned with Offred as an individual. The professor seems more interested in finding out the identity of Offred's Commander. He offers two possible identifications: Frederick R. Waterford, who 'possessed a background in market research' (p. 319), or the more sinister figure of B. Frederick Judd. Offred has already told us that her Commander was in 'market research' (p. 195), but Professor Pieixoto does not seem to regard her words as reliable.

We might view the professor's reconstruction of Offred's story as marking a radical shift from 'herstory' to 'history'. He tries to discredit Offred's narrative by accusing her of not paying attention to important things. He ignores what she wanted to tell – a tale of the suffering and oppression of all women and most men in Gilead. In this way, his presentation erases Offred as a person. He cannot tell his delegates what happened to her because he does not know – but he seems uninterested. Offred's own prediction for her story of the Handmaids was bleak: 'From the point of view of future history … we'll be invisible' (p. 240). Two hundred years later, her words are proved to be true.

The novel ends on a question; we are invited to join in the debate. This is the point at which Atwood's novel assumes the **didactic** tone that distinguishes anti-utopian (**dystopian**) fiction. It moves beyond the confines of a fictional world to become a warning about our own future. It is a future we might choose to avoid.

A03 **KEY CONTEXT**

Atwood has constructed her modern anti-utopia using many references drawn from Western cultural history. There are connections with the Bible and late twentieth-century feminism and environmental issues. There are also references to seventeenth-century American Puritanism, the slave trade, Nazism and pornographic films, as well as **motifs** from fairytales, quotations from Shakespeare, John Milton, René Descartes, Alfred Lord Tennyson, Sigmund Freud and Karl Marx. The 'Historical Notes' add even more references, so that we come to see Gilead as placed in a history of oppression and rule by other totalitarian states.

Revision task 10: The professor   **A02**

Make brief notes about the 'Historical Notes' section, and what they reveal. Write about:

- The professor's perspective on Offred
- The reader's perspective on the professor

Consider whether Offred is erased from her own story by the professor's words, or whether her story survives, and shows her resistance to the Republic of Gilead.

PROGRESS CHECK

Section One: Check your understanding

These tasks will help you to evaluate your knowledge and skills level in this particular area.

1. List three or four key **narrative** techniques that Atwood uses that reveal Offred's inner life and sharpness of mind.

2. Find three or four examples of images from nature used in the narrative.

3. Make a table listing some of the ways in which Gilead uses biblical language.

4. Write a short paragraph explaining how Atwood's narrative uses the female body.

5. Find two examples where Offred's narrative is outward facing, using 'you'. Explain briefly why she might do this.

6. To chart how the Gileadean **dystopia** subjugates women, make a table listing other Handmaids in the novel. For each, add a note about what happens to them.

7. Write brief notes explaining the different stages of Janine's story – the narrative is structured so that she reappears throughout. List two ways in which she is significant in the novel.

8. List four or five of the main features of a dystopian society.

9. Write a short paragraph explaining why you think an author may write dystopian fiction.

10. Write a short paragraph explaining the way the narrative uses **flashback**.

Section Two: Working towards the exam

PROGRESS BOOSTER   A01

For each Section Two task, read the question carefully, select the key areas you need to address, and plan an essay containing six to seven points. Write a first draft, giving yourself an hour to do so. Make sure you include supporting evidence for each point, including quotations.

Choose one of the following three tasks which require longer, more developed answers:

1. 'The Handmaid's Tale is a narrative in which female voices of protest are heard.' To what extent do you agree with this statement?

2. Consider ways in which The Handmaid's Tale might be considered as political and social protest writing.

3. 'I'm sorry there is so much pain in this story. I'm sorry it's in fragments, like a body caught in crossfire' (p. 279). Discuss the ways in which Atwood has chosen to construct and present Offred's story to us.

Progress check (rate your understanding on a level of 1 – low, to 5 – high)	1	2	3	4	5
How the story develops within a framing narrative					
How dialogue contributes to characterisation					
How the text can modify our understanding of the dystopian genre					
The dramatic effect of the mosaic-like, fragmented story					
The use of vocabulary and poetic imagery within the prose narrative					

HISTORICAL CONTEXT

The American New Right

Atwood's clippings file for *The Handmaid's Tale* contains a great deal of material she researched about the American New Right in the early 1980s. It was at this time that religious right-wing fundamentalist groups became a significant political force in America, with their strong backing for President Reagan and the Republican Party. This right-wing Christian movement warned about the 'Birth Dearth' and expressed concern about such matters as the right to abortion, the rise of divorce and the growth of the Gay Rights movement. As a coalition of conservative interests which sought to influence government legislation on family issues and public morals, the New Right looked back to America's Puritan inheritance, and was politically powerful throughout the 1980s under President Reagan and the first President Bush.

Support for the New Right was particularly strong in the south-eastern and south-central areas of the country known as 'Bible Belt' America, where church attendance across all Christian denominations is high and evangelical Christianity is popular. Several prominent women activists were associated with this movement such as Phyllis Schlafly (a possible model for the Commander's Wife) who travelled round the country making speeches and mobilising women to support right-wing policies on gender and family issues.

Puritan New England

Atwood's interest in Puritan New England relates to her own ancestry (especially to her relative Mary Webster, who underwent attempted hanging as a witch in 1683 but survived her ordeal) and also to her studies at Harvard under Professor Perry Miller, the great scholar of the Puritan mind (see 'Dedication and epigraph'). With its passion for traditional values, Atwood's Republic of Gilead borrows selectively from the historical model of the Puritan forefathers of America: 'The mindset of Gilead is really close to that of the seventeenth-century Puritans' (*Conversations*, p. 223). Many of the practices of Atwood's Gilead, especially its attitudes to women as the inferior sex, are reminiscent of the Puritans. For example, Anne K. Kaler writes that New England Puritan women were assigned names like 'Silence, Fear, Patience, Prudence, Mindwell, Comfort, Hopestill and Be Fruitful' so as to be 'reminded … of their feminine destiny', and they were not allowed to use combs or mirrors or wear anything but plain and functional clothing. (From Gina Wisker, *Margaret Atwood: An Introduction to Critical Views of her Fiction*).

Utopian ideals

As Atwood has pointed out repeatedly, the Puritans aspired to a **utopian** society, though the system they evolved was oppressive, theocratic and **patriarchal**. Atwood cites a remark by New England novelist Nathaniel Hawthorne (1804–64) that one of the first things built in Puritan New England was a prison and the second was a gallows to hang dissenters. Atwood sees it as the tragedy of American history that the nation is based on a failed aspiration to build utopia in the New World. In her reading of contemporary American literature, she sees an America haunted by the ghost of that failed inheritance:

> 'Most twentieth-century American literature is about the gap between the promise and the actuality, between the imagined ideal Golden West or the City upon a Hill, the model for all the world postulated by the Puritans, and the actual squalid materialism, dotty small town, nasty city, or redneck-filled outback.' (*Survival*, p. 32)

A03 KEY CONTEXT

In 1979, the Baptist minister and televangelist Jerry Falwell founded the Moral Majority, a movement that brought together and mobilised the support of many Christians and Republicans. Televangelists like Falwell, Pat Robertson and Jim Bakker and Tammy Faye Bakker (who has also been cited as a possible model for the Commander's Wife) were extremely popular in the late 1970s and 1980s.

A03 KEY CONTEXT

In 1983 a collection of essays called 'The New Right at Harvard' edited by Howard Phillips was published. This might at least partly explain why Atwood chose Harvard University as the 'heartland' of Gilead.

It should be added, however, that Atwood draws on a range of international sources to inform her outlook. Not only does Atwood **satirise** American society and history, but Gilead's tyrannical practices are based on international historical models as well as contemporary political atrocities in Latin America, Iran and the Philippines. 'Denay, Nunavit' (p. 311) or 'Deny none of it' seems to be Atwood's message, shocking readers out of complacency into a recognition of our world and of our shared moral responsibility for it.

Revision task 12: Puritan attitudes to women   **A03**

Atwood's university teacher Professor Perry Miller's historical works provide many of the details which are used in the novel, such as Puritan preachers' reference to women as 'Handmaids of the Lord', and many of the practices connected with childbirth, like the birthing stool or the gathering of all the women during labour as witnesses to a birth.

Make notes on how Atwood transposes seventeenth-century behaviour and beliefs into the late twentieth/early twenty-first century, and the effect of this on the reader.

Feminism

Atwood delivers a sobering warning to readers about Gilead's attempts to redefine female identity in reductively biological terms, but the novel also provides a brief history and critique of the North American feminist movement since the 1960s. Offred's memory narrative includes the rise of second wave feminism and the anti-feminist backlash of New Right Christian fundamentalism. The voices of the women in the novel represent a range of traditional feminine and new feminist positions dating back to the Women's Liberation movement of the late 1960s. Offred's mother, a single parent, belongs to this early activist group with its campaigns for women's sexual freedom, its pro-choice rallies and pornographic magazine burnings. Offred comments ruefully on her own indifference to her mother's radical feminist activism and laments the political apathy of so many younger women, which she believes contributed to the rise to power of the extreme right wing. As she now realises, 'We lived as usual, by ignoring. Ignoring isn't the same as ignorance, you have to work at it' (p. 66).

The opponents to feminism are represented in the novel by the Commander's Wife and the Aunts, who show they are more than willing to collaborate with Gilead's regime to re-educate women back into traditional gender roles. Among the Handmaids (younger women who grew up in the 1970s and 1980s), Atwood shows us three very different characters: Janine, who accepts the female victim role; the radical lesbian separatist feminist Moira; and Offred herself, whose story highlights the **paradoxes** and dilemmas within contemporary feminism. As Gilead is quick to point out, women's sexual and economic freedom of choice has brought new anxieties, though the regime's grotesque distortion of the dangerous consequences of feminism discredit their critiques.

Progress booster: Atwood and feminism   **A03**

Atwood identifies herself as a feminist but has spoken about the importance of viewing this word in context. Atwood remarked in 1982, '*Feminist* is now one of the allpurpose words. It really can mean anything from people who think men should be pushed off cliffs to people who think it's O.K. for women to read and write. All those could be called feminist positions. Thinking that it's O.K. for women to read and write would be a radically feminist position in Afghanistan. So what do you mean?' (*Conversations*, p. 140). Think about the characters in the novel in relation to the word 'feminism'. What do we learn about the views held by Moira and by Offred's mother? What does Offred have to say about these views? What is the Aunts' stance on the feminism of 'the time before' (p. 231)?

KEY CONTEXT   **A03**

Some of the heroines of the second wave feminist era were Simone de Beauvoir (*The Second Sex*, translated into English in 1952), Betty Friedan (*The Feminine Mystique*, 1963) and Germaine Greer (*The Female Eunuch*, 1970). Their focus was on women's bodies and female sexuality; on issues around motherhood, abortion and reproductive technologies; pornography and violence against women; and equal pay as well as environmentalism and peace campaigns.

KEY CONTEXT   **A03**

The feminist movement rapidly gained strength in the United States, winning Congressional endorsement of the Equal Rights Amendment (ERA) in 1972 and the Supreme Court decision to make abortion legal in 1973. However, opposition campaigns and lobbying by the New Right and pro-life campaigners meant that the ERA failed to be ratified in 1982, a bitter defeat for feminism. For a useful history of Anglo-American feminism, see *Feminisms: A Reader* (1992), edited by Maggie Humm.

SETTINGS

Writing in 1985, Atwood (a Canadian) set her novel in the near future in what we are led to understand was previously the United States of America. Atwood's depiction of life in the Republic of Gilead is close enough to our time for the **protagonist** to remember the 1970s and 1980s and be at the time of telling her story only thirty-three years old. While some of the features of Gilead could apply to any late twentieth-century or early twenty-first century state with

advanced technology and pollution problems, the location is made explicit in the 'Historical Notes', and also in various places within Offred's narrative. Examples include her description of the Gileadean takeover 'when they shot the President and machine-gunned the Congress' (pp. 182–3), Moira's escape along what she recognises to have once been Massachusetts Avenue or 'Mass Ave.' (p. 257) and the reference to 'July the Fourth, which used to be Independence Day' (p. 209), a federal holiday in America celebrating the Declaration of Independence of 4 July, 1776.

By making references to the USA and by including **flashbacks** to the time before Gilead, Atwood is able both to shock readers and also to **satirise** certain aspects of politics, religious worship, society and culture in modern America. Her setting of her novel in a specific place – her former place of study, Harvard University, and the local area of Cambridge, Massachusetts – creates bitter ironies. In what was once a world-famous seat of learning, literacy and freedom of movement are now seen as dangerous, and Salvagings take place on the very steps where students would once have celebrated their graduation. Atwood strikes a positive note about the enduring value of knowledge and scholarship by setting the 'Historical Notes' in a university environment in the year 2195. Offred's first-person narration and frequent use of flashbacks enable the reader to share Offred's defiance and 'double vision' – viewing locations both as they are and as they were. Offred describes numerous places in painstaking detail, including the Rachel and Leah or Red Centre, and many of the rooms in the Commander's house. Such descriptions convey to the reader the reality of Offred's confined existence and of how her environment affects her.

A03 KEY CONTEXT

In the early twenty-first century, the libertarian Tea Party movement has been an active voice on the American Right. Its name references the 1773 Boston Tea Party, a protest against taxation by the British.

A05 KEY INTERPRETATION

Atwood deliberately leaves the time of her **dystopia** unspecific, though the American critic Lee Thompson cites Atwood's manuscript note which gives Offred's birth date as 1978, which would mean that her adult eyewitness account of life in Gilead belongs to the first decade of the twenty-first century.

LITERARY CONTEXT

The form, **genre** and subject matter of *The Handmaid's Tale* provide useful points of comparison with a wide range of other texts, written both before and after the novel itself.

Dystopian fiction

Set in a futuristic USA at the beginning of the twenty-first century, *The Handmaid's Tale* is an example of **dystopian** fiction. Coral Ann Howells writes that 'the primary function of a dystopia is to send out danger signals to its readers' (*Margaret Atwood*, 1996); in other words to function both as a warning and to some extent as a prophecy based on the author's present concerns about the world around them.

Atwood had read and been inspired by numerous examples of dystopian fiction, ranging from Jonathan Swift's *Gulliver's Travels* (1726) to many twentieth-century novels, including:

- Yevgeny Zamyatin's *We* (1920–1) in which the uniformed inhabitants of One State – including central character D-503 – live in glass buildings to aid surveillance, and are given numbers rather than names
- Aldous Huxley's *Brave New World* (1932) which also expresses grave concerns about the loss of individual identity in the modern world in a story which depicts human reproduction taking place only in 'hatcheries and conditioning centres'
- George Orwell's *Nineteen Eighty-Four* (1949), which describes Winston Smith's life in 'Airstrip One' under the watchful eye of 'Big Brother', the Party leader (for further discussion of *Nineteen Eighty-Four*, see below)
- John Wyndham's 1955 *The Chrysalids,* in which a brutal fundamentalist Puritan society destroys babies with abnormalities in the name of 'Purity of the Race'

A clear parallel can be drawn between Wyndham's novel and Atwood's description of the fate of unfit babies in Gilead, ominously referred to as 'Unbabies' (p. 123) or 'shredder(s)' (p. 226). In fact, perhaps the most significant and the most nightmarish aspect of life in Gilead is the response to the falling birth rate, where reproduction is entirely controlled by the state and Handmaids like Offred are seen as a 'national resource' (p. 75) because of their fertility. P. D. James's dystopian thriller *The Children of Men* (1992) – set in 2021 – also imagines how society and governments would respond to a global infertility crisis, and the prospect of human beings becoming an extinct species.

The environmental and ecological concerns that shape *The Handmaid's Tale* are also central to J. G. Ballard's *The Drowned World* (1962), in which the ice caps have melted and London has become a swamp. The idea of a post-literate future society is famously written about in Ray Bradbury's 1953 dystopian novel *Fahrenheit 451*, and in her novel Atwood also describes a regime that frowns on education and books and where pictures have replaced words on shop signs. Both Atwood's novel and Doris Lessing's *The Memoirs of a Survivor* (1974) feature a female narrator recording her personal perspective on a chaotic futuristic 'outer world' as well as her private 'inner world'.

The Handmaid's Tale and *Nineteen Eighty-Four*

Many of the themes of *The Handmaid's Tale* are to be found in *Nineteen Eighty-Four*. It offers a similar warning against threats of totalitarianism in the not-too-distant future, and presents the ways in which any totalitarian state tries to control not only the lives but also the thoughts of its subjects. Orwell's protagonist Winston Smith lives in a nightmarish world of surveillance with giant television screens and posters declaring 'BIG BROTHER IS WATCHING YOU' as he wanders the London streets or sits at home alone. There are similar efforts to

KEY CONNECTION   A04

One of the most recent examples of the dystopian genre is Cormac McCarthy's 2006 post-apocalyptic novel *The Road*. It was made into a film starring Viggo Mortensen as the father and Kodi Smit-McPhee as the son in 2009.

KEY CONNECTION   A04

Although desire and pleasure have no place in Offred's puritanical official existence, they endure – in the sexual underground of Jezebel's and in Offred's passionate affair with Nick. Atwood writes in an introduction to Aldous Huxley's classic science fiction novel *Brave New World* (1932) that Huxley's imagined society is characterised by 'boundless consumption' and 'officially endorsed promiscuity' because 'sex and procreation have been separated'.

George Orwell

silence opposition at any price, and both novels warn against the dangers of **propaganda** and censorship. Atwood pays particular attention to the abuses of language in Gilead where the meanings of words are changed to their opposites (as in Orwell's 'Newspeak') in an effort to restructure the way people are allowed to think about their world. For example, the Gileadean **rhetoric** of 'Aunts', 'Angels' and 'Salvagings' takes words with reassuring emotional connotations and distorts them into **euphemisms** for the instruments of oppression.

Gilead has a similarly oppressive structure to Orwell's 'Oceania'. However, the two novels come out of different historical contexts and project different futuristic scenarios, with *The Handmaid's Tale* voicing the political, social and environmental anxieties of late twentieth-century capitalist North American culture. Furthermore, Offred's situation and perspective are very different from Orwell's protagonist Winston Smith's. Whereas she is relegated to the political margins of Gilead and confined to domestic spaces as a conscripted Handmaid, where she is forbidden to read and write, Winston Smith reads and writes continually at the 'Ministry of Truth'. He is employed to destroy historical records and to forge new historical 'facts' according to the dictates of the Party propaganda machine. (It would be his job to invent the kind of news reportage that Offred watches on the television in Serena Joy's sitting room.) By contrast, Offred has only the most anecdotal knowledge of how the fundamentalist Gileadean regime came to power or how the system functions. As she says of her Commander, 'I don't know what he's a Commander of. What does he control, what is his field, as they used to say?' (p. 195).

Given Offred's enforced ignorance, Atwood has to explain Gilead's political philosophy and its mechanisms of control via a male voice in the 'Historical Notes', whereas in *Nineteen Eighty-Four* Winston understands the policies of Oceania both through his work and through the forbidden black book that he secretly reads. Indeed, Offred's narrative with its focus on the trivial events of her daily life as she looks for 'tiny peepholes' (p. 31) or fracture lines in the system, appears as a deliberate resistance to Orwell's masculine fascination with institutional politics and military tactics. Atwood's version focuses on those very things that Orwell left out of his dystopia, so that her story shifts the structural relations between the private and public worlds to which Orwell, like his male predecessors, conformed. Instead, Offred's story concentrates on the concerns of the officially silenced others. The endings are different too, for Atwood's novel opens the ambiguous possibility for Offred's escape, whereas there is no escape for Winston Smith or for his lover Julia, who are broken by the system. Winston is brainwashed into loving Big Brother by the end, whereas Offred never comes to love the Commander. Instead, with the help of her lover Nick it appears that she is able to escape from Gilead, though Atwood offers us no certainties in this respect.

Revision task 13: Surveillance **A04**

From the 'Eyes' to the idea of sending the Handmaids out shopping in pairs, surveillance takes many forms in Atwood's Gilead. Make notes on the different forms of surveillance in *The Handmaid's Tale*, and how they compare with the surveillance culture described by Orwell in *Nineteen Eighty-Four*.

A04 **KEY CONNECTION**

Orwell's novel, set in London, was published in the bleak post-war period of the 1940s in the context of the Cold War, the rise of Stalinist terrorism and the building of the Berlin Wall, and pervaded by recent memories of Nazi Germany. He envisages a nightmare Europe by the early 1980s, ruled over by a totalitarian state called Oceania which is committed to terrorism and perpetual war.

A03 **KEY CONNECTION**

Terry Gillam's *Brazil* (1985), a futurist dystopia, offers a black comic parallel to *The Handmaid's Tale*.

William Blake

Political and social protest writing

Atwood's protagonist's form of protest is not loud or outspoken – Offred challenges and satirises the Gileadean regime in numerous ways including her secret thinking, her humour and her memories of the time before. Offred's 'double vision' as her thoughts shift between the past and the terrifying reality of life in Gilead in the present could be compared with William Blake's illustrated collection of poems, *Songs of Innocence and of Experience* (1789). In this collection, Blake compares innocence with experience as a way of protesting at the various ways in which institutions repress and corrupt human nature. Atwood's use of the first-person narrator in her **fictive autobiography** shows how the personal and the political are profoundly connected for Offred. Khaled Hosseini's 2003 novel *The Kite Runner* is a **Bildungsroman** that also weaves together the story of the protagonist Amir and the political systems and events that affect and shape his experiences.

Science fiction

From Mary Shelley's *Frankenstein* (1818) to H. G. Wells's *The War of the Worlds* (1898) and beyond, the science fiction **genre** offers a space to imagine some of the practical and ethical consequences of advances in science and technology, to ask 'what if …?' Atwood refers in her novel to the role played by computerised technology in Gilead and to the power of doctors in assessing Handmaids' fertility, though science and technology do not play as central a part in Atwood's narrative as they do in many other examples of the genre, perhaps because the Gileadean **ideology** may be seen to be a reaction against 'progress' rather than an example of it. In *Frankenstein*, a gifted scientist discovers that he can create life, though in so doing he creates a monster whom society shuns, prompting the monster to take his revenge. In *The War of the Worlds*, Wells considers the consequences of a Martian invasion. All three authors give their narratives specific and recognisable locations known to the authors and many of their readers, making their speculative fictions all the more believable.

Canadian science fiction

There is also a specifically Canadian science fiction context for Atwood's novel. Since the 1960s, other Canadian novelists had been writing about the dangers of nuclear accidents and warning against ecological disaster. The best known are Phyllis Gotlieb, whose *Sunburst* (1964) was set in the near future in Canada; Wayland Drew's *The Wabeno Feast* (1973), which is another scenario of ecological disaster; Michael Coney's *Winter's Children* (1974); and Hugh MacLennan's post-holocaust novel *Voices in Time* (1980). It is Atwood's originality in combining the themes of national disaster with those of Canadian-American relations and a global history of totalitarian oppression, all told from a feminine narrative perspective, which has made *The Handmaid's Tale* such a popular and disturbingly relevant novel.

Atwood's other writings

As Canada's most famous writer and one of the most well-respected novelists writing in English today, Margaret Atwood has been publishing her poetry, prose and criticism since the 1960s. She has experimented with a wide range of narrative genres including Gothic romance, spy thrillers and science fiction. Writing about three of her novels, Atwood has commented that, 'To my mind, *The Handmaid's Tale*, *Oryx and Crake* and now *The Year of the Flood* all exemplify one of the things science fiction does, which is to extrapolate imaginatively from current trends and events to a near-future that's half prediction, half satire' (Guardian, 14 October 2011). It is also useful to view Atwood's prose in the context of her achievements in poetry, both in terms of her writing style and the topics she writes about. Her narrative poem 'Half-Hanged Mary', for example, is about her ancestor Mary Webster, one of the people to whom *The Handmaid's Tale* is dedicated.

KEY INTERPRETATION **A05**

In his essay 'Margaret Atwood in her Canadian context' (in *Margaret Atwood*, 1996), David Staines remarks that 'Perhaps only a Canadian, a neighbour as well as an outsider to the United States, could create such an unsettling vision of the American future'.

CRITICAL INTERPRETATIONS

Critical history

A great deal of attention has been paid to *The Handmaid's Tale* as **dystopian** science fiction (or 'speculative fiction' as Atwood prefers to call it), and as a novel of feminist protest. It has won many prizes, notably the Arthur C. Clarke Science Fiction Prize, and has been made into a film directed by Volker Schlöndorff and starring Natasha Richardson, Faye Dunaway and Robert Duvall (1990). In 2000, Atwood's novel was made into an opera by the Danish composer Poul Ruders, and it has also inspired radio and stage adaptations and a ballet. Yet the novel has provoked criticism in America from the religious right and aroused some debate over Atwood's exposure of the flaws and failures of 'second wave' feminism, especially in her representation of the Aunts and the character of Offred.

However, Atwood is not exclusively concerned with feminist politics but rather with gender politics and with basic human rights. As a consequence of its both its originality and its international success, *The Handmaid's Tale* has become a cultural reference point as it brings into focus many of the anxieties and fears of contemporary Western society in what at times seems a rather prophetic way: 'The book seems ever more relevant in a world of jostling theocracies and diminished civil liberties in both east and west' (*Guardian Review*, 26 April, 2003, p. 23). As one interviewer phrased it in 2001: 'It's almost impossible now to imagine a time when *The Handmaid's Tale* didn't exist.'

Reaction on publication

Looking back to its first publication in 1985, reviews of *The Handmaid's Tale* voiced a conflicting range of responses. Atwood commented that while the book triggered an anxious and nervous reaction among the Canadian media who perceived that Atwood was writing about very real possibilities, the British media did not tend to treat the book as a work of social realism. By contrast, she comments that American reviewers found her novel particularly unsettling and prophetic.

These disparities are reflected in the reviews, as this selection suggests. The first one is Canadian, the second is British, and the last three are American:

- 'In *The Handmaid's Tale*, Atwood's pessimism comes to the fore as she attempts to frighten us into an awareness of our destiny before it's too late' (*Globe and Mail*, 1985).
- 'Atwood's triumph is to capture the eerily static, minute-by-minute quality of Offred's sensations, in a life reduced to a meagre sequence of small incidents and stifled and impoverished human contacts, and seen through a consciousness heightened by waiting and fear' (*London Review of Books*, 1986).
- 'She gives us far too little action and far too much of the longueurs long suffered by the interned Offred' (*USA Today*, 1986).
- 'The novel achieves what it is meant to do, shatters complacency and pulls us up short' (*Detroit Free Press*, 1986).
- '*The Handmaid's Tale* provides a compelling lesson in power politics and in reasonable intentions gone hysteric' (*Philadelphia Inquirer*, 1986).

These reviews map out the initial critical approaches to the novel, with their emphases on genre and gender. However, Offred's first-person narrative was not universally read by early critics as feminist protest but rather as a female victim's cry of desperation, though two male reviewers (one English and one American) did tune in appreciatively to Offred's humorously **ironic** voice:

Margaret Atwood

A04 **KEY CONNECTION**

As well as the Bible, Atwood alludes to many other texts in *The Handmaid's Tale*, such as Nathaniel Hawthorne's story of Puritan New England *The Scarlet Letter* (1850), fairytales like Little Red Riding Hood, Jonathan Swift's social **satire**, *A Modest Proposal* (1729) and a number of popular songs. Atwood has called her novel 'One of the most allusion-studded things I've done' explaining that the novel's title alludes to Chaucer and to the Bible ('On Allusion', *University of Toronto Quarterly*, 61, 3, 1992).

A03 **KEY CONNECTION**

For a listing of manuscript materials relating to *The Handmaid's Tale*, search online for the Thomas Fisher Rare Book Library, University of Toronto.

'Gripping like an intelligent thriller, compelling like all believable **dystopias**, it's also a reply to puritans of left and right, showing how, even in conditions of dire psychic deprivation, people still want and get sex. It's a sign of life, indestructible.' (*New Statesman*, 1987)

and

'Atwood's book is suffused by life – the heroine's irrepressible vitality and the author's lovely subversive hymn to our ordinary life, as lived, amid perils and pollution, now.' (*The New Yorker*, 1986)

KEY INTERPRETATION

See Lee Briscoe Thompson's *Scarlet Letters* for a comprehensive list of quotations from contemporary reviews (pp. 78–82).

Contemporary approaches

Margaret Atwood's writings have been the subject of many critical works. Analysis of *The Handmaid's Tale* has examined Atwood's inventiveness with genre, form, narrative technique and language, and her exploration of power, **ideology**, gender, sexuality and history within the novel, among other topics. Critics have developed interpretations using a range of critical approaches, some of the most influential of which are discussed below.

Feminist criticism

One of the objectives of feminist criticism is to reveal how literary works support or challenge the assumptions of a male-dominated social order or **patriarchy**. Given the subject matter of *The Handmaid's Tale,* its female narrator and the other complex female characters in the novel, a great deal of criticism of this novel can be described as coming from a feminist perspective.

Coral Ann Howells has written about the novel's challenge to the genre of dystopian fiction, arguing that Atwood's 'choice of a female narrator turns the traditionally masculine dystopian **genre** upside down, so that instead of Orwell's analysis of the public policies and institutions of state oppression, Atwood gives us a dissident account by a Handmaid who has been relegated to the margins of political power' (*Margaret Atwood*, 1996).

Another genre-related angle has been to consider how Atwood challenges the romance genre, while at the same time alluding to some of the conventions and familiar tropes of that genre; the critic J. Brooks Bouson writes about how Atwood presents femininity as a construct and how she, in the words of commentator Heidi Slettedahl Macpherson, subversively 'unpicks the fantasy of romantic love' (from *The Cambridge Introduction to Margaret Atwood*, p. 116). Feminist criticism has also addressed issues including female sexuality, the relationships between mothers and daughters and between men and women, how the feminist movement is represented in the novel, and the role and portrayal of the Aunts. Pilar Somacarrera writes about how the Aunts' power 'is disguised as a spirit of camaraderie' (in *The Cambridge Companion to Margaret Atwood*, 2006) 'similar to that of the army' and Marta Dvorak writes about how Offred uses 'caricature' to portray the Aunts, as an act of resistance (*Lire Margaret Atwood*, 1999).

Progress booster: Writing the body

A significant focus for close analysis has been Offred's poetic descriptions of her body, her sensations and her desires, with some critics alluding to Hélène Cixous's pioneering essay 'The Laugh of the Medusa' (reprinted in *New French Feminisms*, ed. E. Marks and I. de Courtivron) as they explore Offred's interior monologues and the importance of body language within Gilead's publicly enforced female silence. Following Cixous, critics like Thompson, Howells, Karen Stein (*Margaret Atwood Revisited*, 1999), and Michael Greene in his essay 'Body/Language in *The Handmaid's Tale*: Reading Notes' (*Lire Margaret Atwood*, 1999) comment on Offred's poetic language. They analyse her creative use of **metaphor** and her lyrical imagery of flowers and the natural processes of growth and fertility within the novel, all signalling a traditionally feminine response to experience and creating what has been called 'the seductive erotics of romantic narrative'. Through her interior monologue Offred continually reminds herself, not only of the past but of her individuality in the present, which exceeds Gilead's definition of her as a 'two-legged womb' (p. 146). From her own perspective Offred's body is more like a wilderness or a dark cosmic landscape, the site of her desires and longings for love or for her grief over the loss of all her family.

Psychoanalytic criticism

The neurologist Sigmund Freud (1856–1939) developed the discipline of psychoanalysis, which suggests that human behaviour is to a large extent determined by desires and drives of which we are unconscious. He suggested that we may become aware of these desires and drives through indirect means such as dreams or slips of the tongue. As well as Freud, concepts from the psychoanalytical theories of Jacques Lacan and Carl Jung have also been very influential in the study of literary texts – concepts relating to the unconscious, the psyche, sexual theory and the interpretation of dreams. Critics who have drawn on these ideas have been able to explore Atwood's creation of complex, multi-dimensional characters in her fiction, such as Offred, whose story has many strands and moves fluidly between the past and the present. Eleonora Rao has drawn on these ideas, particularly Lacanian psychoanalytical theories, and applied them to Atwood's exploration of ideas about home, the self, memory, borders and exile in relation to numerous works by Atwood (*Strategies for Identity: The Fiction of Margaret Atwood*, Peter Lang, 1993). Shannon Hengen's *Margaret Atwood's Power: Mirrors, Reflections and Images in Select Fiction and Poetry* (1993) also offers psychoanalytical readings of Atwood's work.

Literary critics taking a psychoanalytical approach to *The Handmaid's Tale* might point to the recurring 'Night' sections in order to investigate Offred's expressions of her hopes, fears, memories and desires in these private periods of reflection. For example, Offred's failed escape with her husband Luke and their daughter is recalled and re-imagined on several occasions, a **flashback** that Coral Ann Howells refers to as Offred's 'one central traumatic memory' with 'jagged edges'. Other interesting areas for close analysis are Atwood's references to 'mirrors' (and their absence in Gilead), and the **motif** of the 'double'.

A03 KEY CONTEXT

Conflicting interpretations of – and ongoing debates about – this novel testify to its relevance in changing contemporary contexts. As Atwood explained: 'You cannot determine people's reactions to your book. If it's a book with any power, there's always going to be some form of uproar' (from *Margaret Atwood, The Essential Guide* by Jonathan Noakes and Margaret Reynolds, Vintage Living Texts, 2002).

Foucauldian criticism

Michel Foucault (1926–84) was a French philosopher, historian of ideas and social theorist whose ideas relating to power, knowledge, language, society and sexuality have been extremely influential in a range of fields including literary criticism. In *Discipline and Punish: The Birth of the Prison* (1975), Foucault wrote about torture, punishment, discipline and prison, and argued that modern society creates 'docile bodies' by means of surveillance and by people's internalisation of 'disciplinary individuality', and thus the dominant ideology seems increasingly 'natural'. In her essay 'Power politics: power and identity', Pilar Somacarrera writes that 'Given that *The Handmaid's Tale* depicts the quintessential disciplinary society where power is brought to the most minute and distant elements, Foucault's model can be applied to almost all of its aspects'. Somacarrera quotes Aunt Lydia – 'The Republic of Gilead … knows no bounds. Gilead is within you' – and cites a number of examples of the methods by which the 'Gileadean regime … aims to be ubiquitous and internalized by the population' including 'brainwashing and strict surveillance undertaken by security forces: the Angels (army), the Eyes ("invisible" police), and the Guardians' as well as the power of doctors over reproduction and 'torture for political dissenters'. Heidi Slettedahl Macpherson also describes how the Republic of Gilead functions in her description of 'overt mechanisms for control, fear of betrayal and inculcated self-surveillance' (*The Cambridge Introduction to Margaret Atwood*, pp. 53–54).

New Historicist criticism

'New Historicism', a term coined by critic Stephen Greenblatt, approaches literary texts not as privileged works of art that stand outside of history but as documents that may be read in conjunction with non-literary texts in order to produce critical understanding of particular historical moments and cultural contexts. Foucault's teachings were a major influence on this movement and, with its view that history is an incomplete record and the value New Historicism places on previously marginalised texts and voices, it can be viewed as a **postmodern** approach to textual interpretation.

It could be argued that *The Handmaid's Tale* was conceived and written in a way that is extremely conscious of such an approach to texts. Atwood collected in a clippings file an assortment of texts such as newspaper articles that reflected the issues and debates that interested and concerned her in the 1980s. *The Handmaid's Tale* also contains several fragments of other texts, from nursery rhymes and pop songs to prayers and hymns, as a way of remembering and reflecting on culture from the past and as part of Offred's resistance to the Gileadean ideology of the present day. Atwood's novel is in itself a disempowered voice from the margins of history – albeit, of course, a fictitious one – and in the novel's 'Historical Notes' Atwood playfully demonstrates how 'official' histories come into being. The critic Coomi S. Vevaina describes Pieixoto as 'interested in reconstructing his grand impersonal narrative of a vanished nation's history' and comments that Offred's 'narrative status diminishes considerably in Pieixoto's reconstruction of her story' (from 'Margaret Atwood and History' in *The Cambridge Companion to Margaret Atwood*, p. 87). Throughout Offred's narrative itself, however, Atwood continually reminds the reader to view storytelling as an inadequate reconstruction and to resist the idea that there can be one objective view of history – to 'deny none of it'.

PROGRESS CHECK

Section One: Check your understanding

These tasks will help you to evaluate your knowledge and skills level in this particular area.

1. In what ways does *The Handmaid's Tale* reflect political and religious developments in the USA in the 1980s? Make brief notes.

2. Write a paragraph about *The Handmaid's Tale* in the context of the science fiction genre and/or other dystopian novels.

3. What should we infer from Offred's description of the Commander's house and garden about the Commander and the Commander's wife? List three key points.

4. Make a table listing at least three points of connection between *The Handmaid's Tale* and another literary text you have studied.

5. List three to four events or situations that might provide focal points for a feminist reading of this novel.

6. How is the dominant ideology in Gilead enforced? List three or four ways and include specific references to the text.

7. To what extent would you describe *The Handmaid's Tale* as a 'multi-voiced narrative'? Write a paragraph explaining your viewpoint.

8. What kind of insights might be gained from a new historicist reading of *The Handmaid's Tale*? Make brief notes.

9. Write a paragraph explaining how a critical work you have read has enhanced your understanding of the relationship between language and power within this novel.

10. Refer to three extracts from the novel in which Offred writes about the human body, and make references to relevant critical perspectives.

Section Two: Working towards the exam

1. Consider the significance of surveillance in *The Handmaid's Tale* and in any other dystopian novel you have studied.

2. 'There is no power without resistance.' What different kinds of resistance feature in Atwood's novel?

3. How does Atwood make use of debates about the methods and objectives of the second wave feminist movement in her novel?

A01 PROGRESS BOOSTER

For each Section Two task, read the question carefully, select the key areas you need to address, and plan an essay containing six to seven points. Write a first draft, giving yourself an hour to do so. Make sure you include supporting evidence for each point, including quotations.

Progress check (rate your understanding on a level of 1 – low, to 5 – high)	1	2	3	4	5
How some knowledge of context enhances interpretation of the novel					
The different ways the novel can be read, according to critical approaches such as feminist or New Historicist					
How comparison with another literary work can deepen understanding of both					
How a reader's interpretation may differ from the author's intended meaning					
How *The Handmaid's Tale* can be read as a historical document					

ASSESSMENT FOCUS

How will you be assessed?

Each particular exam board and exam paper will be slightly different, so make sure you check with your teacher exactly which Assessment Objectives you need to focus on. You are likely to get more marks for Assessment Objectives 1, 2 and 3 if you are studying AQA A or B, but this does not mean you should discount 4 or 5. Bear in mind that if you are doing AS Level, although the weightings are the same, there will be no coursework element.

What do the AOs actually mean?

	Assessment Objective	Meaning
A01	Articulate informed, personal and creative responses to literary texts, using associated concepts and terminology, and coherent, accurate written expression.	You write about texts in accurate, clear and precise ways so that what you have to say is clear to the marker. You use literary terms (e.g. 'imagery') or refer to concepts (e.g. 'oppression') in relevant places. You do not simply repeat what you have read or been told, but express your own ideas based on in-depth knowledge of the text and related issues.
A02	Analyse ways in which meanings are shaped in literary texts.	You are able to explain in detail how the specific techniques and methods used by Atwood to create the text (e.g. **narrative** voice, **dialogue**, **flashback**) influence and affect the reader's response.
A03	Demonstrate understanding of the significance and influence of the contexts in which literary texts are written and received.	You can explain how the text might reflect the social, historical, political or personal backgrounds of Atwood or the time when the novel was written. You also consider how *The Handmaid's Tale* might have been received differently over time.
A04	Explore connections across literary texts.	You are able to explain links between the *The Handmaid's Tale* and other texts, perhaps of a similar **genre**, or with similar concerns, or viewed from a similar perspective (e.g. feminist).
A05	Explore literary texts informed by different interpretations.*	You understand how *The Handmaid's Tale* can be viewed in different ways, and are able to write about these debates, forming your own opinion. For example, how a critic might view female voices as raised in protest, while another might see women as muted by the **patriarchal** views that endure.

* AO5 is not assessed by Edexcel in relation to *The Handmaid's Tale*.

What does this mean for your revision?

Whether you are following an AS or A Level course, use the right-hand column above to measure how confidently you can address these objectives. Then focus your revision on those aspects you feel need most attention. Remember, throughout these Notes, the AOs are highlighted, so you can flick through and check them in that way.

Next, use the tables on page 85. These help you understand the differences between a satisfactory and an outstanding response.

Then, use the guidance from page 86 onwards to help you address the key AOs, for example how to shape and plan your writing.

Features of **mid-level** responses: the following examples relate to Offred's role in the novel.

Features	Examples
A01 You use critical vocabulary appropriately most of the time, and your arguments are relevant to the task, ordered sensibly, with clear expression. You show detailed knowledge of the text.	*Offred narrates her story using flashbacks, particularly in the 'Night' sections. This means we gradually learn about her past life, and the loved ones she has lost.*
A02 You show straightforward understanding of the writer's methods, such as how form, structure and language shape meanings.	*When Offred is alone, the reader becomes aware of her inner voice, which uses imagery to reveal her love of life.*
A03 You can write about a range of contextual factors and make some relevant links between these and the task or text.	*The idea of a dystopian society is important in the novel, but it is also a feminine dystopia, as Offred is a female storyteller in a male-dominated society.*
A04 You consider straightforward connections between texts and write about them clearly and relevantly to the task.	*In Gilead, Offred is forced to use a different language, for example when she greets other Handmaids, or attends a Prayvaganza. This is similar to George Orwell's 'Newspeak' in* Nineteen-Eighty Four – *in both novels language is changed into an instrument for control.*
A05 You tackle the debate in the task in a clear, logical way, showing your understanding of different interpretations.	*Some would argue that Offred is powerless and unable to act, but it could equally be said that she uses the small 'peepholes' in Gileadean society to resist the regime.*

Features of a **high-level** response: these examples relate to a task on narrative technique.

Features	Examples
A01 You are perceptive and assured in your argument in relation to the task. You make fluent, confident use of literary concepts and terminology, and express yourself confidently.	*Offred's inner life is demonstrated in the intense, lyrical quality of the prose. The private language of her inner self is filled with rich imagery and reveals Offred's entirely different perception of herself as a woman and her world. In contrast, her external voice is muted and bland; disconnected from emotion.*
A02 You explore and analyse key aspects of Atwood's use of form, structure and language and evaluate perceptively how they shape meanings.	*The novel opens in palimpsestic form, where Offred's present is overlaid with story from her remembered past. Her memories of the gym are 'green-streaked', 'felt-skirted' and filled with 'the pungent scent of sweat' as colour, texture and aroma are recovered from lost moments of her history. Even as we begin to understand her new, bleak present, we are drawn into her past.*
A03 You show deep, detailed and relevant understanding of how contextual factors link to the text or task.	*Atwood's own understanding of the dystopian form is demonstrated in the way she manipulates it, handing the storytelling to a woman struggling to survive in a brutal patriarchy. As Atwood admits herself, it may 'surprise the reader'. What surprises and thrills us is the feminised language of resistance in Offred's narrative voice which results.*
A04 You show a detailed and perceptive understanding of issues raised through connections between texts. You use a range of excellent supportive references.	*Atwood uses the overt symbolism of the Eye as state surveillance; Like Orwell's 'Big Brother', Gilead disguises its more sinister aspects as state protection. Gilead's soldiers are Guardian Angels and it is ironic that, while* Nineteen-Eighty Four *depicted a world of futuristic telescreens, Atwood's dystopia draws on ancient Scripture for its vision of the future.*
A05 You are able to use your knowledge of critical debates and the possible perspectives on an issue to write fluently and confidently about how the text might be interpreted.	*Offred's story is recovered far into a future where she no longer exists, and a feminist viewpoint would see this as symbolic of women's voices raised in protest against patriarchy. But the professor's speech in the 'Historic Notes' can be seen as reductive. Does Offred's story endure, or is her voice of protest ultimately erased?*

HOW TO WRITE HIGH-QUALITY RESPONSES

The quality of your writing – how you express your ideas – is vital for getting a higher grade, and **AO1** and **AO2** are specifically about **how** you respond.

Five key areas

The quality of your responses can be broken down into **five** key areas.

1. The structure of your answer/essay

- First, get **straight to the point in your opening paragraph**. Use a sharp, direct first sentence that deals with a key aspect, and then follow up with evidence or a detailed reference.
- **Put forward an argument or point of view** (you won't **always** be able to challenge or take issue with the essay question, but generally, where you can, it is more likely to make you write in an interesting way).
- **Signpost your ideas** with connectives and references that help the essay flow. Aim to present an overall argument or conceptual response to the task, not a series of unconnected points.
- **Don't repeat points already made**, not even in the conclusion, unless you have something new to add.

> **EXAMINER'S TIP**
>
> AO1 and AO2 are equally important in AS and A Level responses.

Aiming high: Effective opening paragraphs

Let's imagine you have been asked about Offred's **narrative** voice. Here's an example of a successful opening paragraph:

> Gets straight to the point

> One of the chief concerns in a dystopian society is the control of body and mind, but ultimately we come to view Offred's narrative voice as one that seeks freedom from the strict conditions of control imposed upon her. As the narrative unfolds we learn of her grief and anguish – how does she achieve psychological and emotional freedom under a regime that would erase her identity? How does she deal with the loss of her loved ones and, as Offred reveals more of her past how do we come to view her voice as resisting, or even actively engaging in rebellion?

> Sets up some interesting ideas that will be tackled in subsequent paragraphs

2. Use of titles, names, etc.

This is a simple, but important, tip to stay on the right side of the examiners.

- Make sure that you spell correctly the titles of the texts, chapters, authors and so on. Present them correctly too, with inverted commas and capitals as appropriate. For example, 'The Handmaid's Tale'.
- Use the **full title**, unless there is a good reason not to (e.g. it's very long).
- Use the term 'text' rather than 'book' or 'story'. If you use the word 'story', the examiner may think you mean the plot/action rather than the text as a whole.

3. Effective quotations

Do not 'bolt on' quotations to the points you make. You will get some marks for including them, but examiners will not find your writing very fluent.

The best quotations are:

- Relevant and not too long (you are going to have to memorise them, so that will help you select shorter ones!)
- Integrated into your argument/sentence
- Linked to effect and implications

Aiming high: Effective use of quotations

Here is an example of an effective use of a quotation about the role of gender politics in the novel:

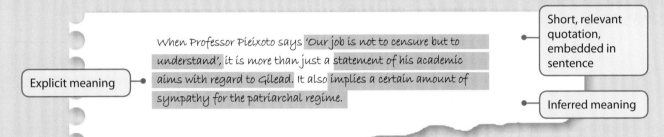

Explicit meaning

When Professor Pieixoto says 'Our job is not to censure but to understand', it is more than just a statement of his academic aims with regard to Gilead. It also implies a certain amount of sympathy for the patriarchal regime.

Short, relevant quotation, embedded in sentence

Inferred meaning

Remember – quotations can also be one or two single words or phrases embedded in a sentence to build a picture or explanation, or they can be longer ones that are explored and picked apart.

4. Techniques and terminology

By all means mention literary terms, techniques, conventions, critical theories or people (for example, 'paradox', 'archetype', 'feminism' or 'Plato') **but** make sure that you:

- Understand what they mean
- Are able to link them to what you're saying
- Spell them correctly

5. General writing skills

Try to write in a way that sounds professional and uses standard English. This does not mean that your writing will lack personality – just that it will be authoritative.

- Avoid colloquial or everyday expressions such as 'got', 'alright', 'OK' and so on.
- Use terms such as 'convey', 'suggest', 'imply' or 'infer' to explain the writer's methods.
- Refer to 'we' when discussing the audience/reader.
- Avoid assertions and generalisations; don't just state a general point of view ('Serena Joy's character is unfeeling – she hates Offred and is corrupt') but analyse closely with clear evidence and textual detail.

Note the professional approach here in the choice of vocabulary and awareness of the effect on the reader:

Atwood **conveys** *a sense of a character who, each time the Ceremony takes place, endures her own private pain. As readers* **we** *are compelled to feel an increasing sense of Serena Joy's helpless anguish as we consider Offred's question: 'Which of us is it worse for?' (p. 106).*

> **EXAMINER'S TIP**
>
> Something examiners pick up on is that students often confuse 'narrator' and 'author'. Remember that Offred is a character as well as the narrator, and don't confuse her with the novel's author, Margaret Atwood.

QUESTIONS WITH STATEMENTS, QUOTATIONS OR VIEWPOINTS

One type of question you may come across is one that includes a statement, quotation or viewpoint from another reader. You are likely to be asked this about *The Handmaid's Tale*, or about *The Handmaid's Tale* and another text you have studied.

These questions ask you to respond to, or argue for/against, a specific **point of view** or critical interpretation. Your question is likely to be in relation to the theme of modern times or the **genres** of political and social protest writing or **dystopia**.

For *The Handmaid's Tale* these questions will typically be like this:

> **'A corrupt society will have as its main concerns the balance of power, and elimination of resistance.' Examine this view of Atwood's presentation of the Republic of Gilead in *The Handmaid's Tale*.**

The key thing to remember is that you are being asked to **respond to a particular perspective or critical view** of the text – in other words, to come up with **your own** 'take' on the idea or viewpoint in the task.

Key skills required

The table below provides help and advice on answering the question above.

Skill	Means?	How do I achieve this?
To focus on the specific aspect, by exploring Atwood's authorial methods	You must show your understanding of the genre, first tackling the ways in which 'power' and 'elimination of resistance' are key concerns in a dystopian society, and secondly deciding how this applies to Gilead.	You will need to deal with the issue generally, either in an opening paragraph or in several paragraphs, but also make sure you keep on coming back to this issue throughout the essay, rather than diverting into other areas that you have not been asked about.
To consider different interpretations	There will be more than one way of looking at the given question. For example, critics might be divided about the extent to which the Commander is presented as a victim of a corrupt system.	Show you have considered these different interpretations in your answer. For example, a student might write: *The Commander's power feeds his belief that he is immune and does not prevent him from taking advantage of Offred. He is perhaps symbolic of the corruption of Gilead – yet ultimately he is also an isolated figure controlled by the regime.*
To write with a clear, personal voice	Your own 'take' on the question is made obvious to the examiner. You are not just repeating other people's ideas, but offering what **you** think.	Although you may mention different perspectives on the task, you settle on your own view. Use language that shows careful, but confident, consideration. For example: *Although the Commander may be seen as a symbol of power in a corrupt system, I feel that he is powerless as his attempt to break away from his designated role leads to his own undoing.*
To construct a coherent argument	The examiner or marker can follow your train of thought so that your own viewpoint is clear to him or her.	Write in clear paragraphs that deal logically with different aspects of the question. Support what you say with well-selected and relevant evidence. Use a range of connectives to help 'signpost' your argument. For example: *We might say that the Commander's role is symbolic of corrupt power.* **However**, *the freedoms he provides for Offred are powerful in themselves.* **Furthermore**, *they become small 'peepholes' through which she can exercise rebellion.*

Answering a 'viewpoint' question

Let us look at another question:

> **'The central protagonist's voice is one of many raised in protest yet silenced by the patriarchy of Gilead.'**
>
> **To what extent do you agree with this view? Remember to include in your answer relevant detailed exploration of Atwood's authorial methods.**

Stage 1: Decode the question

Underline/highlight the **key words**, and make sure you understand what the statement, quotation or viewpoint is saying. In this case:

'To what extent do you agree …' means: *Do you wholly agree with this statement or are there aspects of it that you would dispute?*

'Central protagonist' means: *leading character in the story*

'raised in protest' means: *speaking out against unfairness*

'patriarchy' means: *a system or government in which men hold the power*

So you are being asked whether you agree or disagree with the view that Atwood's male-dominated dystopian society excludes women from making their views heard, or having any power.

Stage 2: Decide what your viewpoint is

Examiners have stated that they tend to reward a strong view which is clearly put. Disagreeing strongly can lead to higher marks, provided you have **genuine evidence** to support your point of view. However, don't disagree just for the sake of it.

Stage 3: Decide how to structure your answer

Pick out the key points you wish to make, and decide on the order that you will present them in. Keep this basic plan to hand while you write your response.

Stage 4: Write your response

Begin by expanding on the aspect or topic mentioned in the task title. In this way, you can set up the key ideas you will explore. For example:

Atwood imagines a near-future world where brutal, male-dominated systems of government leave women with little or no power. It could be argued that Offred, subject to the strict rules of Gilead and defined only by her role as Handmaid, is mute; her life is reduced to mere survival. But her narrative voice would indicate otherwise …

Then in the remaining paragraphs, proceed to set out the different arguments or perspectives, including your own.

In the final paragraph, end with a clear statement of your viewpoint, but do not list or go over the points you have made. End succinctly and concisely.

EXAMINER'S TIP

You should comment concisely, professionally and thoughtfully, and present a range of viewpoints. Try using modal verbs such as 'would', 'could', 'might' and 'may' to clarify your own interpretation. For example, *I would argue that to say Offred's voice is a protest heard by those in the future is largely untrue. Professor Pieixoto's speech may be viewed as dismissive in tone, with the result that her woman's protest is perhaps reduced and undermined by his patronising treatment of her story.*

COMPARING *THE HANDMAID'S TALE* WITH OTHER TEXTS

As part of your assessment, you may have to compare *The Handmaid's Tale* with or link it to other texts you have studied. You may also have to link or draw in references from texts written by critics.

Linking or comparison questions might relate to a particular theme, **genre** or idea, such as science and society or **dystopian** fiction. For example:

> **Compare the ways in which the writers of your two chosen texts present scientifically advanced societies or societies filled with doubts and fears. You must relate your discussion to relevant contextual factors.**

Or:

> **Much dystopian fiction explores a futuristic world of controlled misery. By comparing *The Handmaid's Tale* with at least one other text prescribed for this topic, discuss how far you agree with this view.**

You will need to:

Evaluate the issue or statement and have an **open-minded approach**. The best answers suggest meaning**s** and interpretation**s** (plural):

- For example, in relation to the first question: do you agree that doubts and fears may be features of an advanced society? Do both texts demonstrate this? How?
- What are the different ways in which this question or aspect can be read or viewed?
- What evidence is there in each text for this perspective? How can you present it in a thoughtful, reflective way?
- What are the points of similarity and difference?

Express **original or creative approaches** fluently:

- This isn't about coming up with entirely new ideas, but you need to show that you're actively engaged with thinking about the question, not just reeling off things you have learnt.
- **Synthesise** your ideas – pull ideas and points together to create something fresh.
- This is a linking/comparison response, so ensure that you guide your reader through your ideas logically, clearly and with professional language.

Know ***what* to compare/contrast**: the writer's methods – **form**, **structure** and **language** – will **always** be central to your response. Consider:

- The authorial perspective or voice (who is speaking/writing), standard versus less conventional narration (use of **flashback**, **palimpsest**, disrupted time or **narrative** voice which leads to dislocation or fragmentation)
- Different characteristic use of language (lengths of sentences, formal/informal style, dialect, accent, balance of **dialogue** and narration; difference between prose treatment of an idea and poem)
- Variety of **symbols**, images, **motifs** (how they represent concerns of author/time; what they are and how and where they appear; how they link to critical perspectives; their purposes, effects and impact on the narration)
- Shared or differing approaches (to what extent do Atwood and the author(s) of Text 2/3 conform to/challenge/subvert approaches to writing about fear?

EXAMINER'S TIP

Remember that for the AQA A or B specifications in order to score highly in your answer you will also need to discuss what the critics say (AO5) and consider relevant cultural or contextual factors (AO3). AO5 is not assessed by Edexcel in relation to *The Handmaid's Tale*.

Writing your response

Let us use the example from page 90:

> **Compare the ways in which the writers of your two chosen texts present scientifically advanced societies or societies filled with doubts and fears.**

Introduction to your response

- Either discuss quickly what 'scientifically advanced societies or societies filled with doubts and fears' means, and how well this applies to *The Handmaid's Tale* and the other text you have studied, or start with a particular moment from one of the texts which allows you to launch your exploration.

- For example, you could begin with a powerful quotation to launch your response:

'Dear God, I think, I will do anything you like.' Offred's internal narrative voice prays for life in a world that is so full of threat and fear that she doubts she will survive – yet she yearns to go on living. It is her bleak and perilous existence that has brought her to this point, for Atwood has created a dystopian society which has at its core deception, brutality and constant danger of death.

Main body of your response

- **Point 1:** Continue your exploration of fear and danger in Offred's life: the threats to her survival, the way the Republic of Gilead maintains control over its subjects and what this implies about totalitarian systems of government. Refer to Atwood's concerns about Western society at the time of writing – how might we view these issues differently?

- **Point 2:** Now cover a new factor or aspect through comparison or contrast of this issue with another in Text 2. For example, *Shelley, in Frankenstein, creates an 'Abhorred monster' of her own in the unnamed Creature, which reflects the fears and doubts of the period of Romanticism and the potential inability of the human mind to grasp scientific advancement.* How is this idea in Text 2 presented **differently or similarly** by the writer according to language, form and structures used; why was it done in this way?

- **Points 3, 4, 5, etc.:** Address a range of other factors and aspects, for example other ways in which fear is used, **either** within *The Handmaid's Tale* **or** in both *The Handmaid's Tale* and Text 2. What different ways do you respond to these – and why? For example:

> **EXAMINER'S TIP**
>
> If you are following an AS course, you may have less exam time to write than for the A level – so concise, succinct points with less elaboration than provided here may be needed.

Gilead uses torture and death as instruments of control through constant fear. The bodies of the men hanging on the Wall are a disturbing dramatic tableau of death, and what the reader finds most ominous is that they are perhaps symbolic of every man: their identity is stripped away as they hang with 'their heads in white bags'. The bodies wear white coats and so it seems that doctors – those at the forefront perhaps of scientific advance – have become 'war criminals' of the new regime. Offred here reverts to her coping mechanism where her narrative 'detaches' and 'describes': 'What they are hanging from is hooks' – a statement given more emphasis by the use of alliteration, simple lexis and lack of adjectives to soften. The sinister image of hanged men and detached description work powerfully on us as readers as we share the horror of a potential future filled with mortal fear.

Conclusion

- Synthesise elements of what you have said into a succinct final paragraph.

In 'Frankenstein', Shelley focuses the fears and doubts of an uncomprehending society in her nightmare creation, or corruption of science. Her Gothic creature remains, perhaps, in the realm of the fantastical. However, in 'The Handmaid's Tale', Atwood is more concerned with corrupt systems of government which, in her speculative dystopian vision are perhaps all the more disturbing and fearful because of their potential to exist in our own reality.

USING CRITICAL INTERPRETATIONS AND PERSPECTIVES

What is a critical interpretation?

The particular way a text is viewed or understood can be called an interpretation, and can be made by literary critics (specialists in studying literary texts), reviewers, or everyday readers and students. It is about taking a position on particular elements of the text, or on what others say about it. For example, you could consider:

1. Notions of 'character'

What **sort/type** of person Offred – or another character – is:

• Is the character an 'archetype' (a specific type of character with common features)?

The critic Lynette Hunter has suggested that Atwood is concerned with the actions of one person within a system of control, so that rather than focusing on Gilead, the novel's main focus is Offred herself and her individual actions in resisting control.

• Does the character **personify**, **symbolise** or represent a specific idea or trope (a moderate feminist; one model of a hero)?

• Is the character modern, universal, of his/her time, historically accurate, etc.? (For example, can we see elements of what we might consider a more dated idea of feminism in Offred? Does her narrative construct a language that draws on more traditional ideas of what is 'feminine', such as nature, and the female body?)

2. Ideas and issues

What the novel tells us about **particular ideas or issues** and how we interpret these. For example:

• How society is structured: the Republic of Gilead in the Handmaid's Tale is modelled on the hierarchical structure of a totalitarian state. This means that the novel scrutinises the way that absolute power remains in the hands of the few while the masses are controlled by systems which often lead to misery.

• The role of men/women: there have been several major feminist movements in our recent history. The 'Historical Notes' reveal however that a patriarchal, male-dominated social order remains in place far into the future and that Offred's words of protest remain, finally, unheard.

• Moral codes and social justice: the greatest **irony** of Gilead perhaps is that it purports to follow a moral code laid down in the Scriptures, yet in practice Handmaids such as Offred are subjected to systematic rape and denial of all freedoms – social justice has been swept aside and replaced with social control.

3. Links and contexts

To what extent the novel **links with, follows or pre-echoes** other texts and/or ideas. For example:

• Offred's story might be compared with Charlotte Perkins Gilman's protagonist in *The Yellow Wallpaper* (1892), who becomes institutionalised by her confinement. Like Offred, Jane's narrative is highly imaginative and she is a natural storyteller.

- The way Atwood creates a society which rules through fear might be compared with H. G. Wells's *War of the Worlds* (1898), which scrutinises the way we behave as a group when faced with fear. In contrast, Atwood's focus remains with the plight of the individual.
- Elements of Offred's blinkered existence might be compared to the restricted life that Sylvia Plath's protagonist, Esther, endures in *The Bell Jar* (1963), a comment on 1950s American society's expectations of women.

4. Genre and narrative structure

How the novel is **structured** and how Atwood constructs her narrative:

- Does it follow particular narrative conventions? For example, those of the **dystopian genre**?
- What are the functions of specific events, characters, plot devices, locations, etc. in relation to narrative or genre?
- What are the specific moments of tension, conflict, crisis and **denouement** – and do we agree on what they are?

5. Reader responses

How the novel **works on the reader**, and whether this changes over time and in different contexts:

- How does Atwood **position** the reader? Are we to empathise with, feel distance from, judge and/or evaluate the events and characters?

6. Critical reaction

And, finally, how do different readers view the novel? For example, different critics over time, or different readers from the 1990s to more recent years.

Writing about critical perspectives

The important thing to remember is that **you** are a critic too. Your job is to evaluate what a critic or school of criticism has said about the elements above, arrive at your own conclusions, and also express your own ideas.

In essence, you need to: **consider** the views of others, **synthesise** them, then decide on **your perspective**. For example:

Valuable insights might be gained from a Marxist reading of the text where systems of power in the Gileadean society are scrutinised and power bases are constructed through mechanisms of control. In contrast, a feminist reading will highlight the voice of the individual woman who speaks out, even when marginalised in a rigid patriarchy. I feel that both viewpoints suggest that capitalist societies are inherently corrupt. The 'Historical Notes' are evidence that little perhaps changes: the powerful remain in control, and those who exercise less power, whether women or Orwell's 'proles' in 'Nineteen-Eighty Four', remain peripheral and largely ignored.

A05 KEY INTERPRETATION

Here are just two examples of different responses to *The Handmaid's Tale*:

Critic 1: Like others, Michael Greene, in his essay 'Body/Language in The Handmaid's Tale: Reading Notes', analyses the poetic aspects of Offred's narrative voice as a feminine response, creating a 'romantic narrative'.

Critic 2: Lee Briscoe Thompson, in *Scarlet Letters*, positions the novel as **postmodern**, where Offred is a self-conscious narrator, aware of the relationship between herself as storyteller and the reader as receiver of her story.

ANNOTATED SAMPLE ANSWERS

Below are extracts from three sample answers at different levels to the same task/question. Bear in mind that these responses may not correspond exactly to the style of question you might face– for example, AO5 is not assessed by Edexcel – but they will give a broad indication of some of the key skills required.

> **Question: 'In *The Handmaid's Tale*, Atwood is primarily concerned with the power of the individual rather than any one group or gender.' To what extent do you agree with this view? Remember to include in your answer relevant detailed exploration of Atwood's authorial methods.**

Candidate 1

AO3
Early reference to context – would be better embedded in argument

'The Handmaid's Tale' was written in the 1980s when Margaret Atwood was concerned with Western capitalist American society – at this time the American liberal society was threatened by the rise of a right-wing movement. It is therefore a political novel as well as the story of one individual and therefore I will focus on the novel as concerned with a political group.

'The Handmaid's Tale' is also a social and political protest novel, so it is about how groups may protest and even rebel. For example: there are many groups in the novel, such as Handmaids and Commanders' Wives. The Handmaids have a very restricted life, where they are made to wear uniforms and they have no power in the Gilead society. But in reality they find ways to communicate, for example when Offred goes shopping with Ofglen they communicate using their eyes: 'She holds my stare in the glass, level, unwavering'. This shows us how, even in a society which is ruled by fear and violence, groups may find ways to communicate in secret. It could be the first, small step towards a rebellion.

AO1
Focused, simple approach to interpretation

Another way the groups find ways to communicate is at the Birth Day. For example, Offred says: 'you can find things out, on Birth Days'. The Handmaids come together for the Birth ceremony and use these small whisperings to get messages to each other. The point is, even in a totalitarian state there will be opportunities for groups to resist, perhaps in what Offred calls the 'small peepholes of the state'. Even if it appears that groups have no power, there will be ways in which they resist even the strictest of rules.

AO1
Straightforward argument, supported by textual reference

The Mayday resistance group is important in the novel as this demonstrates the way that groups can come together and become organised. The regime of Gilead rules by using torture and its people live in constant danger, but it appears that the more oppressive a state, the more its people will find ways to resist – perhaps like the French Resistance in the Second World War.

AO3
Simple reference to context

The Salvagings are significant as they are opportunities for the state to demonstrate its supreme power. For example, Offred says: 'Women's Salvagings are not frequent. There is less need for them. These days we are so well behaved'. As stated earlier, the state rules through torture and danger, so the group events become extremely important as they are ways to control. The images of the women who are hanged are powerful deterrents for anyone considering rebellion. The Particicution is a barbaric step further than this, because the Handmaids come together as a group to kill and maim. This is an example of the way the state makes criminals of them all so there is a feeling that they belong. Also, the Handmaids feel that because they are allowed to kill, they have some power after all, and it is a sinister idea that a state can control its subjects by allowing them to act violently, rather than by being peaceful.

AO2

More developed argument with implicit understanding of significance of narrative structure

The most terrifying thing in Gilead is the random nature of the violence. This is also an effective way for the state to control, and is one way the state controls individuals as well as groups. For example when the black van arrives in the street, the Eyes beat up and take away a man. Offred says: 'What I feel is relief. It wasn't me'. We know that Offred is too scared to support the resistance because she says: 'I will do anything you like'. She says this when she realises that Ofglen didn't betray her. This shows how effective the state strategy of rule by fear is because she now understands that it is more important for her to survive than to become an informant. She says: 'I feel, for the first time, their true power'. The state violence has a numbing effect where people are just relieved that it wasn't them. The effect of this is that a policy of random, targeted violence isolates and separates and therefore may weaken groups of resistance fighters.

AO1

Slight loss of focus – recovers by the end of the paragraph

The last group I wish to discuss is men, because Gilead is a good example of male heads of state controlling other men. It is easy to see women as the victims but actually many men are victims in the novel, too, and we can see how the state takes power from individuals such as the Commander and Luke (who is captured and probably killed). The Commander is ironic because he is one of the leaders, but he becomes arrogant, believing he is above the new 'justice' of Gilead. He breaks the rules with Offred and pays for this, probably with his life as he is finally 'a security risk, now'.

AO1

Better here – accurate use of terminology to support comment and uses an embedded quote

In conclusion, I think that the novel examines the way that groups behave when under pressure from a strict ruling power that uses methods of fear and violence to control. This includes men in addition to women, and the most sinister aspect of Gilead is the way that the power of the state separates people from groups so that they are reduced to surviving – or not – as individuals.

MID LEVEL

Comment

- **AO1** A straightforward approach which succeeds in keeping the argument focused most of the time. Some use of terminology. Supported with textual references but not fully explored or analysed.
- **AO2** Shows some understanding of narrative structure, although this is implicit, and a lack of detailed language analysis.
- **AO3** Succeeds in referring to context, though this would be better embedded in argument.
- **AO4** No mention is made of any connection with other literary texts, although makes connections across the novel.
- **AO5** Refers to interpretation – this could have been more developed.

To improve the answer:

- Include some analysis of language and literary techniques and the way meaning is shaped. **AO1**, **AO2**
- Engage more closely with historical and literary context, embedding this in the argument rather than using it as an introduction. **AO3**, **AO4**
- Explore different critical interpretations related to the novel. **AO5**

Candidate 2

By calling her novel 'The Handmaid's Tale', Atwood is inviting us as readers to recognise that her book is the story of one woman and her efforts to survive in a strict society that restricts all her freedom. Offred has very little power in her new existence as a Handmaid in Gilead. Early in the novel, she reveals to us how imprisoned she is: 'I can sit in the chair, or on the window seat, hands folded'.

As the story of one woman, much of the novel is concerned with Offred's story of her everyday life, and how monotonous and restricted this is. During these sections, Offred's own voice is subdued and she is careful to restrict herself to small observations: 'I walk along the gravel path'.

When alone, Offred uses her own power of memory: she uses flashbacks from her past to bring her husband, daughter and best friend Moira to life once more, always hoping they may have survived. This is one of the ways in which she gains strength and comfort. In particular, with memories of her mother and Moira to support her, she feels as if life is worth living and this sustains her through many of the more difficult moments of her life – they both lend her a personal power to keep going. Moira refuses to disappear from Offred's story as she returns to the Rachel and Leah Centre, and then again in Jezebel's. Moira's reappearance gives us insights into the range and intensity of emotion that Offred feels: at the Red Centre with Moira, she feels 'ridiculously happy'. Later at the brothel when they meet again, she weeps as she recognises how desperate their situation has become. She may be filled with delight at seeing her old friend, but we also understand the pain behind their meeting.

The most painful flashbacks are the broken stories of Luke, Offred's husband, and her daughter, and Offred's true grief shows in these moments. Again, we have a sense of this as a personal story – her feelings of loss are overwhelming. Offred tells three different stories of what happened to Luke as she is desperately hoping he has survived, even while deep inside she understands that it is unlikely that he is still alive. These are some of the most personal moments of her story and she is not alone, for all the women with her have their own stories of loss. This could be a story for all those women who are suffering in Gilead, and who lose their lives. But Atwood always said that 'It's the story of one woman under this regime, told in a very personal way'.

Offred describes Luke in great pain, imprisoned and filthy: 'He finds it painful to move his hands, painful to move'. These are images which are heart-rending and a torture for her. Her third version, where he escapes, is one which she uses to comfort herself as she needs to continue hoping. But her remembrance of her husband is perhaps tinged with guilt here, because just before this she has been with Nick and has felt attracted towards him. These complex feelings make Offred's story all the more human and personal.

A02 Good focus and fair point, supported with textual reference, though this needs further analysis to show depth of understanding

A02 Useful quote; could be analysed further

A02 Good point and accurate reference to narrative technique

A01 Insightful point, though phrasing is a little awkward

A02 Good insight into Moira's function

A03 Useful reference to context, but could be more clearly drawn out

A05 Personal interpretation, but lacking critical angle

Because this is the story of one woman's experience, the reader is very sympathetic towards Offred and concerned to know her fate, but she does not reveal whether she is handed over to the spies, or whether she escapes with the resistance fighters: 'And so I step up, into the darkness within; or else the light'. We know from the 'Historical Notes' that her story has survived, but we do not know whether she has, herself, so there are several different possible outcomes for Offred; a postmodern understanding of the world is that we can construct our own, different realities. God's Word has been abused by the Republic of Gilead in its twisted use of biblical language, so in a way the novel points to there being no religion to save Offred. This could be the author's own comment, as Atwood was a postmodern writer, so instead of a prescribed happy ending we are left to wonder what happened to Offred.

AO3
> Focused argument here on context, though less confident

Offred's personal story finally becomes a romance. She turns to love, and finds it in her relationship with Nick. We can even view the ending as a typical romance where the 'knight in shining armour' saves the damsel in distress. Right at the last moment, Nick says 'It's all right ... Go with them ... Trust me'. But if *The Handmaid's Tale* is the story of one woman, it can also be viewed as a feminist story, and thus relates to the power of gender of all women, to some extent, as Offred does not lose her composure with the guards. Offred's mother was herself a feminist – we know she was a member of the Women's Liberation Movement and campaigned for equality for women. She could therefore be symbolic of the proactive political activism of the 1970s. By seeing her mother in films at the Red Centre, and knowing how desperate her own, new, life is, Offred finally realises that her mother's freedom in active feminism was right – at least she could make a stand, whereas Offred now has no power to speak out at all.

AO5
> Brings in a different interpretation

AO3
> Succeeds in bringing in a reference to context and extending discussion of different interpretation, although a bit clumsily with slight loss of focus

But this remains a story of individuals – here, a mother and her daughter. During the novel, as Offred relives her memories of her mother, she comes to realise that instead of being embarrassed by her, she loved and admired her: 'we didn't do badly by one another, we did as well as most'.

GOOD LEVEL

Comment

- **AO1** A well-focused, thorough response which shows accurate written expression with only a few slips into awkwardness. Well supported by textual references.
- **AO2** Shows good understanding of how meaning is shaped through narrative structure.
- **AO3** Succeeds in discussing context, though this feels a little tacked on.
- **AO4** Explores connections within and across the whole text but does not refer to other texts.
- **AO5** Succeeds in discussing a feminist viewpoint, though rather clumsily.

To improve the answer:

- Analyse and explore author's use of language and its effect in more depth – achieve 'critical distance' by referring to what the **author** has done, rather than the **character**. **AO1, AO2**
- Widen argument to include other texts. **AO4**
- Embed different interpretations more effectively into argument. **AO5**

Candidate 3

A01 A strong, confident opening with close focus on question

We might ask: if Atwood is concerned with the power of the individual, why did she create a female protagonist with so little power? Under the totalitarian rule of Gilead, Offred is in a position of powerlessness and every move risks torture and/or death. Her identity has been stripped away and she is physically confined inside her Handmaid's red uniform, her view restricted by the white wings of her headdress. Her wider and more sensory understanding of the world is reduced to the sphere of the small – the bland and domestic.

Powerless though she may appear, however, Offred finds moments of freedom as she exploits the 'small peepholes' in the regime through which she can exercise a subversive power. The Gilead state may have erased her identity, but she finds ways to recover and re-establish her individual Self. Atwood structures the narrative as a palimpsest: Offred's bleak present is overlaid with remembered story, and this is one of the ways in which the text reveals her resistance to the regime as the narrative shifts between the present and remembered past. Offred's internal voice recovers her loved ones so that we come to see her not merely as isolated in her present, but as an individual grounded in her own history of loved ones.

A01 Assured tone with confident use of textual references to support point

A01 Perceptive analysis of language to support confident discussion

In the 'Night' sections, Offred says, 'But the night is my time out. Where should I go? She recalls Moira with 'purple overalls, one dangly earring, the gold fingernail ... stubby yellow-ended fingers'. Offred's former world of her individual Self is reconstructed. In contrast to the bland, distanced prose of the daytime descriptions, the use of detail here is rich as the close attention to colour reincarnates Moira in the present moment. Returned to the present, Offred 'detaches' and 'describes': 'I lie, then, inside the room ... behind the white curtains, between the sheets'. The text leaves us with a vivid sense of life as her former Self, and thus her as an individual.

Offred's inner narrative voice also possesses a lyrical quality which demonstrates her life and resistance. She refuses the erasure; she <u>insists</u> on being: 'The scent from the garden rises like heat from a body, there must be night-blooming flowers, it's so strong'. The sensual quality of the prose here is far removed from the bleak mono-talk of Gilead. The use of simile, where garden scents and flowers are given a sensual quality, is reinforced in the soft tones of sibilance. The language is alive; it flourishes.

A02 Exploring by now – sophisticated expression and depth of analysis to support

The Handmaid's Tale, however, is not just the story of one woman. Its potential as protest fiction means we can view it as Atwood's social comment or critique. The novel examines the balance of power and powerlessness and those who rebel against a corrupt society; this may reflect Atwood's own concerns about capitalist, Western (American) society, and the specific location of Gilead supports this. One element of the political backdrop to Atwood's writing is the New Right movement of the 1980s, and a feminist reading of the novel would view the fundamentalist patriarchal ideology of Gilead and its constant referencing of Scripture as mirroring the alarming Puritan ideology that was causing anxiety in the United States during the 1980s and which sought to restrict women to the confines of the domestic.

A03 Thoughtful reference to context, well embedded in argument

We may attribute different models of rebellion to other characters: Ofglen's role is as a heroic resistance fighter, while Moira's model is in her refusal to submit. Even in the grotesque tableau of the brothel, her outfit is a cynical comment on the traditional 'Bunny Girl' costume, where 'one breast is plumped out and the other one isn't' and 'one of the ears has lost its starch or wiring and is flopping halfway down'. The shared reference of Moira's costume here may also lead us to interpret the novel as Atwood's cynical comment on patriarchal systems that may underpin Western society and have at their core the denigration of women. The text, then, becomes not about one woman, but many women, and a feminist viewpoint would see the narrative in terms of the stories it has to tell of many women's protests.

A05
Astute reference to a critical perspective

The Gilead state attempts to erase women, but they refuse to disappear. Other, hidden stories are revealed in the stories of other Handmaids, such as Janine, who loses her mind; Ofcharles, of whom we know nothing except that she is hanged; and the unnamed woman who inhabited Offred's room before her, of whom only her scratched words and the Commander's own fragment of story of her fate remains. These women are silenced but we still hear their voices.

A Marxist reading, however, would view the novel as one which scrutinises the balance of power, and the Commander is symbolic of those individuals who, in the division of power, are corrupt themselves – much like the Orwellian pigs in 'Animal Farm'. As Offred comments at the brothel: 'He's breaking the rules, under their noses ... getting away with it'. Serena Joy's own model of corruption is to coerce – to have a child, she arranges secret meetings between Offred and Nick, and thinks nothing of bribing Offred with the possibility of a photograph of her lost daughter.

A04
Useful literary reference

Offred's inner voice is a means for the emotional survival of the individual in a world turned most brutal. But what is perhaps most compelling is the way that the narrative constructs a female voice of power. Atwood's use of vivid imagery from nature and the female body resurrects a female voice in a patriarchal system of government: 'the irises, rising beautiful and cool on their tall stalks, like blown glass, like pastel water momentarily frozen in a splash, light blue, light mauve'. The poetic quality of the language here is enriched by assonance ('tall stalks'), similes ('like blown glass, like pastel water') and soft consonants, and it is alive with colour. The text constructs a feminised language of nature which resists Gilead's attempts at control in its oppressive, twisted language.

A01
Perceptive analysis of language to support confident discussion

A01
Accurate use of terminology to support perceptive analysis

But if we reposition the text as a social/political critique, the novel becomes a comment on corrupt systems of (patriarchal) government and their fallibility – by the end of the novel we know that the Republic of Gilead has been swept away. Power may corrupt, but it may not endure.

Comment

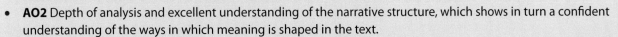

VERY HIGH LEVEL

- **AO1** An impressively coherent and personal response. Consistently accurate use of terminology with sophisticated expression and critical distance.
- **AO2** Depth of analysis and excellent understanding of the narrative structure, which shows in turn a confident understanding of the ways in which meaning is shaped in the text.
- **AO3** Focused engagement with context, which is well embedded in the argument.
- **AO4** Connections to other literary texts used with precision.
- **AO5** Confident and assured reference to critical approaches and the light they might shed on central issues of the text.

PRACTICE TASK

Now it's your turn to work through an exam-style task on *The Handmaid's Tale*. The key is to:

- Quickly read and decode the task/question
- Briefly plan your points – then add a few more details, such as evidence, or make links between them
- Write your answer

Decode the question

> As an example of political and social protest writing, a major concern of *The Handmaid's Tale* is the rebellion of the individual against systems of power. To what extent do you agree with this view in relation to the novel?

'As political ... protest writing'	What are the main ideas behind political and social protest writing and where does rebellion fit in?
'rebellion of the individual'	Are there individuals who resist, or rebel? Who?
'systems of power'	Are the rules imposed by the government, or state?
'To what extent do you agree?'	What is my view? Do I agree with the statement completely, partially or not at all?

EXAMINER'S TIP

Use critical sources to inform your reading of the text, but remember the most important interpretation is your own!

Plan and write

- Decide your viewpoint
- Plan your points
- Think of key evidence and quotations
- Write your answer

Success criteria

- Show your understanding of **political and social protest writing** as a genre
- Draw on a range of critical views or different interpretations as appropriate
- Sustain your focus on the idea of 'rebellion'
- Argue your **point of view** clearly and logically
- Make perceptive points and express your ideas confidently
- Support your points with relevant, well-chosen evidence including quotations
- Use literary terminology accurately and appropriately with reference to the effect on the reader
- Write in fluent, controlled and accurate English

Once you have finished, use the **Mark scheme** on page 112 to evaluate your response.

PART SEVEN: FURTHER STUDY AND ANSWERS

FURTHER READING

Margaret Atwood, *Second Words: Selected Critical Prose*, Anansi, 1982. Reprinted 1996

Contains important Atwood essays on 'Witches' and 'Canadian-American Relations: Surviving the Eighties'

Margaret Atwood, *Good Bones*, Virago, 1993

Margaret Atwood, *Eating Fire: Selected Poetry 1965–1995*, Virago, 1998

This collection contains the 'Orpheus' and 'Eurydice' poems

Nathalie Cooke, *Margaret Atwood: A Biography*, ECW Press, 1998

See Chapter 19, which discusses the writing and reception of *The Handmaid's Tale*

Alexander Cruden, *A Concordance to the Old and New Testaments*, ed. C. S. Carey, Routledge, 1925

Indispensable tool for tracing biblical references. Or check the Searchable Web Bible: http://www.gospelcom.net/bible

Maggie Humm, ed., *Feminisms: A Reader*, Harvester-Wheatsheaf, 1992

Useful anthology for the history of Anglo-American feminism since the 1960s

Earl G. Ingersoll, ed., Margaret Atwood, *Conversations*, Virago, 1992

Contains valuable Atwood interviews on *The Handmaid's Tale*; well indexed

Naomi Klein, *No Logo*, Flamingo, 2000

A factual book on the dangers of consumerist society

Krishan Kumar, *Utopianism*, Open University, Press, 1991

Comprehensive overview of this science fiction genre

Elaine Marks and Isabelle de Courtivron, eds, *New French Feminisms: An Anthology*, Harvester-Wheatsheaf, 1981

Contains essay by Hélène Cixous, 'The Laugh of the Medusa'

Pam Morris, *Literature and Feminism*, Blackwell, 1993

Accessible introduction to feminist literary theory and criticism

George Orwell, *Nineteen Eighty-Four*, Penguin, any edition

Important model for Atwood's dystopia

Ruth Robbins, *Literary Feminisms*, Macmillan, 2000

Useful introduction to women's writing and related theoretical issues

Heidi Slettedahl Macpherson, *The Cambridge Introduction to Margaret Atwood*, Cambridge University Press, 2010

Colin Smith, 'Iranian Prisons', *Observer* (6 June, 1984)

Contains eyewitness account of Iranian prison conditions, comparable with Gilead's scenarios

Rosemary Sullivan, *The Red Shoes: Margaret Atwood Starting Out*, 1998

This entertaining biography focuses on Atwood's formative years in the 1970s

Critical studies

Marta Dvorak, ed., *Lire Margaret Atwood: The Handmaid's Tale*, Presses Universitaires de Rennes, 1999

Contains important Atwood lecture, '*The Handmaid's Tale*: A Feminist Dystopia?' and Priscilla Ollier-Morin's essay on American Protestant fundamentalism

Dominick Grace, '*The Handmaid's Tale*: Historical Notes and Documentary Subversion,'

Science Fiction Studies 25, Part 3 (November 1998), pp. 481–94

This essay analyses how the 'Historical Notes' as a male historian's reconstruction forces re-evaluation of Offred's tale

Coral Ann Howells, *Margaret Atwood*, Macmillan, 1996

See Chapter 7 for discussion of *The Handmaid's Tale* as science fiction in the feminine

Coral Ann Howells, ed., *The Cambridge Companion to Margaret Atwood*, Cambridge University Press, 2006

This recent collection contains essays on Atwood's dystopian visions and on power politics in *The Handmaid's Tale*

Linda Hutcheon, *The Canadian Postmodern: A Study of Contemporary English-Canadian Fiction*, Oxford University Press, 1988

See Chapter 7, which discusses Atwood's fiction as Canadian, feminist and postmodernist

B. Johnson, 'Language, Power and Responsibility in *The Handmaid's Tale*: Towards a Discourse of Literary Gossip', *Canadian Literature* 148 (Spring 1996), pp. 39–55

This essay highlights the power of gossip as language of a women's subculture in Gilead

David Ketterer, *Canadian Science Fiction and Fantasy*, Indiana University Press, 1992

Contains a brief discussion of *The Handmaid's Tale* as a 'contextual dystopia'

J. M. Lacroix and J. Leclaire, eds, *Margaret Atwood: The Handmaid's Tale / Le Conte de la servante: The Power Game*, Presses de la Sorbonne Nouvelle, 1998

Essays on survival, psychoanalysis and Atwood's narrative strategies in this novel; six of the nine essays are in English

J. M. Lacroix, J. Leclaire and J. Warwick, eds, *The Handmaid's Tale: Roman Protéen*, Université de Rouen, 1999

See informative interview and round table with Atwood on the genesis of *The Handmaid's Tale;* six of the seven essays are in English

Colin Nicholson, ed., *Margaret Atwood: Writing and Subjectivity*, Macmillan and St Martin's Press, 1994

This contains excellent essays by Mark Evans on the Puritan background to *The Handmaid's Tale*, and by Sherrill Grace on the genre of fictive autobiography

Reingard M. Nischik, ed., *Margaret Atwood: Works and Impact,* Camden House, 2000

This important collection contains essays setting *The Handmaid's Tale* in context, by Coral Howells on genre, and by Lorna Irvine on recycling culture in Gilead

Karen Stein, 'Margaret Atwood's Modest Proposal: *The Handmaid's Tale*', *Canadian Literature*, 148 (Spring 1996), pp. 57–73

This essay examines the different genre conventions employed in the narrative

Karen Stein, *Margaret Atwood Revisited*, Twayne, 1999

This is a critical study and overview of Atwood's works in the Twayne's Authors series

Lee Briscoe Thompson, *Scarlet Letters: Margaret Atwood's The Handmaid's Tale*, Toronto, ECW Press, 1998

Close study of important aspects of the novel in the Canadian Fiction series

Katherine Viner, 'Double Bluff', *Guardian* (16 September, 2000), pp. 18–27

Interview with Atwood on publication of *The Blind Assassin*

Sharon R. Wilson, *Margaret Atwood's Fairy Tale Sexual Politics*, University of Mississippi Press, ECW Press, 1994

This explores Atwood's use of folk tales, fairy tales and legends to give a cultural context for her female storytellers

Sharon R. Wilson, ed. *Margaret Atwood's Textual Assassinations: Recent Poetry and Fiction*,

Ohio State University Press, 2003

These ten essays cover all genres, paying close attention to postmodern, postcolonial and deconstructive features of Atwood's writings

Lorraine York, ed., *Various Atwoods: Essays on the later poems, short fiction, and novels*, Anansi, 1995

See essays by Glenn Willmott comparing the novel and the film version, and by Nathalie Cooke on Atwood's use of the confessional novel genre

It's worth watching the film version of *The Handmaid's Tale*, available on video. Compare and contrast the novel and the film, investigating reasons for their differences

LITERARY TERMS

analogy a parallel word, thing, or idea, used for comparison

Bildungsroman a novel in which the protagonist grows, learns and matures; a 'coming of age' narrative

counter-discourse resistance that takes the form of written or spoken communication

denouement the final part of the story, the drawing together of plot strands at the end of a work of literature, a final resolution or revelation

didactic intended to teach, particularly moral values

discourse written and spoken communication; the French philosopher and social theorist Michel Foucault wrote extensively about the relationship between discourse and power

double an *alter ego* who bears an uncanny partial resemblance to the self and reveals aspects of the self which have been repressed; in consequence, this 'double' seems both familiar and alien

dystopia anti-utopia, the opposite of **utopia** (an ideal imagined world); invented futuristic nightmare world based on current social, political, economic and environmental trends and warning against their possible disastrous implications

écriture feminine feminine writing, a term borrowed from French feminist theory about signs of gender in writing; it refers to highly **metaphorical**, often unpunctuated flowing writing which represents female body processes and emotional rhythms

elegy a reflective work of literature in response to a death, a lament for the dead

epigraph quotation usually found at the beginning of a book, or chapter of a book

euphemism a more pleasant or polite word or phrase used to conceal something unpleasant

fictive autobiography the life story of someone written by him- or herself, which is an invention of the imagination, and not fact

flashback narrative technique which disrupts the time sequence by introducing an event or memory which happened in the past prior to the present action of the novel

genre a type of literature, e.g. historical romance, detective novel or science fiction

ideology a set of ideas and beliefs found in a particular culture and in the texts produced by that culture

irony covert sarcasm; saying one thing while meaning another; using words to convey the opposite of their literal meaning; saying something that has one meaning for someone knowledgeable about a situation and another meaning for those who are not; incongruity between what might be expected and what actually happens; ill-timed arrival of an event which had been hoped for

metaphor figure of speech in which a descriptive term, name or action characteristic of one object is applied to another to suggest a likeness between them, but which does not use 'like' or 'as' in the comparison

motif a recurrent element which is significant in the overall structure of meaning in the text

narrative a story or account of events, real or imagined

neologism the name for a new word or phrase that may be in the process of becoming accepted into mainstream language

oxymoron two elements placed together that appear to be contradictory

palimpsest originally a manuscript on which the writing has been partially erased but is still visible when written over again (invaluable in historical research). It has come to mean a much-amended and revised text

paradox a statement that seems self-contradictory; something which seems absurd or unbelievable, yet which may be true

parody a humorous or ludicrous imitation of a piece of serious writing or speech

patriarchy a social system in which the power of men and women is unequal, with men holding more power in terms of government, property and inheritance, etc.

personification where human qualities are given to animals, objects or ideas

postmodern as literary practice, refers to contemporary writing which self-consciously draws attention to its own **rhetorical** techniques and narrative artifice, so disrupting conventions of realism, commenting 'metafictively' on writing as process, challenging the borderlines between fact and fictions, and problematising the relation between creative writing and critical commentary

propaganda literature, often polemical, designed to persuade a reader or audience to adopt a given cause

protagonist the central character of the novel or narrative

pun the often humorous use of a word or phrase to suggest more than one of its possible meanings, e.g. 'There is a Bomb in Gilead' (p. 230) plays on the closeness in sound but difference in meaning between 'bomb' and 'balm'

rhetoric grandiloquent or affected speech that is often lacking in sincerity or content

satire literature that explores vice or folly and makes them appear ridiculous; usually morally censorious

self-conscious narrator narrator who reveals to the reader that the story is a fabrication, and who comments within the text on the storytelling process in order to emphasise the gap between fiction and reality

symbol something that by association in thought comes to represent something else; often an object that represents something abstract, such as an idea, quality or condition

REVISION TASK ANSWERS

Task 1: A puritanical life AO1

- She describes her simple, standard-issue clothing, including 'full sleeves', 'red shoes, flat-heeled', 'red gloves' and a skirt that is 'ankle-length' (p. 18). In style the clothing sounds rather puritanical, though the colour stands in contrast to the sober colours associated with Puritans.

- Her clothing has connotations of modesty in its coverage of the body and 'wings … keep us from seeing but also from being seen' (p. 18).

- Offred also refers to simple homemade furnishings such as 'a rug … of braided rags'. She says that 'folk art, archaic, made by women' (p. 17) is favoured by the powers that be – 'a return to traditional values'.

- There are also various suggestions in these first chapters that Offred's function in Gilead has religious significance, as she draws a parallel with 'a nunnery' (p. 18) in Chapter 2, and Ofglen and Offred greet each other in Chapter 4 using phrases from the Bible.

Task 2: A key motif AO2

- The doubling motif is established with the reference to the pairs of Handmaids walking together. The uneasy partnership between Wife and Handmaid is a key feature of the Ceremonies and Birth Days.

- The structure of Atwood's narrative moves fluidly between Offred now and the woman she was – perhaps named 'June' (p. 14) – in her pre-Gilead existence.

- A kind of double vision is also a key form of resistance to Gileadean propaganda for Offred, such as when she is at the Wall in Chapter 6 and stresses the importance of 'making … distinctions' (p. 43).

- Yet another kind of doubling takes place when she thinks about the suffering of another person, for example when she wonders 'Which of us is it worse for, her [Serena Joy] or me?' (p. 106), or the 'ordinary-looking man' who is taken by force in the street: 'What I feel is relief. It wasn't me' (p. 179).

Task 3: First-person narrative AO2

- The use of the first person and the disempowered status of the narrator mean that we see events from the perspective of an otherwise silent and marginal character.

- We learn private and intimate details about Offred's life and we also come to understand the risks and dangers of the life she is forced to lead.

- It is a troubling narrative, and Offred is frequently reminded of pain and trauma from her past, particularly in relation to the loss of her daughter and husband, and her ignorance of their fates.

- These shifts between past and present create a psychological realism and help to make Offred's testimony all the more believable and sympathetic.

- The professor's sometimes dismissive treatment of this narrative in the 'Historical Notes' may comes as a shock to the reader, after having read and been affected by the narrator's story.

Task 4: Laughter AO2

- The need to make a 'Noise' (p. 156) is in contrast to Offred's extremely careful and quiet use of spoken language, e.g. 'We learned to lip-read' (p. 14) and 'she hoped I would never have the occasion to call her anything at all' (p. 25).

- In Chapter 15, she also has to repress laughter when Serena Joy begins to cry: 'I feel, as always, the urge to laugh, but not because I think it's funny' (p. 101).

- Laughter in these examples could be seen to symbolise resistance, a desire to escape the customs and conventions that control every aspect of everyone's lives in Gilead.

- In a flashback in Chapter 10, Moira is associated with uninhibited laughter: 'We'll all pee our pants laughing' (p. 66) and in Chapter 31, Offred says 'Moira laughed; she could always do that' (p. 212).

Task 5: Violence AO1

- When two Eyes take a man away in a black van, the incident is described as brutal but also as something that is clearly state-sanctioned rather than criminal, and everything 'resumes as if nothing has happened' (p. 179).

- Atwood gives us further glimpses of violence becoming an everyday reality when she describes the bodies on the Wall, or the public executions and mob violence of Chapters 42 and 43.

- Occasionally, Offred's thoughts turn to violence, such as when she imagines what she could do with a 'knife', 'shears', a 'match' or the 'cutting edges' of a small electric fan (p. 180). Moira on the other hand acts on such thoughts in Chapter 22, when she threatens Aunt Elizabeth with a 'long thin pointed lever' (p. 140) from a toilet.

Task 6: Despair and hope AO2

- Offred's narrative can swing between moments of despair and hope. In Chapter 18, Offred says she simultaneously believes different outcomes in relation to what has happened to her husband Luke: 'Whatever the truth is, I will be ready for it' (p. 116).

- She also describes at the end of this chapter the words 'In Hope' on a headstone – but by contrast her hopes relate not to an afterlife but to the survival of her slim hopes in this life. By wondering 'Does Luke hope?' (p. 116) she implicitly hopes that he is still alive.

- Small details of Offred's existence can give her hope. The upright, overtly sexual and sensual flowers in Serena Joy's garden delight her, as do moments of defiance 'so small as to be undetectable' which she likens to 'the candy I hoarded, as a child' (p. 31).

- The strong characters of Moira, Ofglen and Offred's mother are capable of instilling in Offred feelings of pride and hope – but the unfortunate endings to these characters' stories bring about further despair.

Task 7: Janine AO1

- In Chapter 13, Offred recalls Janine 'Testifying ... about how she was gang-raped at fourteen and had an abortion' (p. 81).
- In Chapter 22, Offred describes Janine not as a 'true believer' in Gileadean ideology but as a weak and troubled character: 'like a puppy that had been kicked too often ... she'd roll over for anyone, she'd tell anything' (p. 139).
- Atwood describes Janine's/Ofwarren's pride in her pregnancy and what it represents: 'She's a magic presence ... She's a flag on a hilltop ... we too can be saved' (p. 36).
- The Birth appears to go well but the baby, Angela, makes little noise, and Offred later hears from Ofglen that the baby was a 'shredder' (p. 226).
- Janine is described as a sorry figure at the Prayvaganza and by the time of the Particicution it is clear that she has suffered a serious decline.

Task 8: Remembering and forgetting AO2

- Atwood presents Offred's narrative as having been constructed from fragments of memories, and she presents Offred's honesty in trying to piece together an imperfect 'reconstruction' of events.
- Many memories from 'the time before' impinge on Offred's present thoughts, particularly in the 'Night' sections.
- Offred experiences a fear of treasured memories fading, memories of her daughter – 'She fades. I can't keep her here with me' (p. 73) – and memories of Luke – 'Day by day, night by night he recedes, and I become more faithless' (p. 281).
- Offred also comments that on a broader scale, memories of a 'time before' will cease to exist and that for future generations of girls 'they'll always have been silent' (p. 231).

Task 9: Offred's life in Gilead AO2

- Offred lives in fear and isolation, never able to forget her own circumstance as a Handmaid: *Give me children, or else I die* (p. 71).
- Offred finds ways to practise subversion. She recounts small moments where she feels the urge to steal something. The scratched words of the previous occupant of her room give her 'a small joy' (p. 62).
- The chief strategy Offred uses to keep herself psychologically strong is to tell stories from her past. These 'memory stories' keep her loved ones from the past with her.
- Offred's emotional survival lies in her love affair with Nick.
- Fear is the greatest driver in Gilead. When she fears she has been betrayed, Offred is reduced to pleading for her life. Her aim is merely to stay alive.

Task 10: The professor AO2

- The professor is a male historian who seems to think Offred is an untrustworthy narrator and doubts the reliability of her story: 'why did she not make her story public?' (p. 323).

- He appears to lack interest in who she was: 'what else do we know about her ... Not very much' (pp. 317–18).
- His presentation goes into great detail when considering the possible identity of the Commander.
- The professor therefore seems intent on devaluing Offred's tale – her identity is erased from her story, fulfilling her own prophecy that her tale would remain invisible in history.
- Offred's voice survives, however, even if it comes to us in a provisional form 'based on some guesswork' (p. 314), and her narrative shows how she resisted the tyranny of Gilead.

Task 11: Offred's capacity for life AO2

- Offred refuses to view herself in flattened terms of function rather than a person, as Gilead would redefine her.
- Offred's resistance shows subversively in her language, for example in her word play.
- Offred's capacity for life bubbles to the surface in her Scrabble games with the Commander.
- The poetic language of Offred's body reveals her inner self as full of life.
- The narrative uses a rich mix of imagery from nature which reveals Offred's energy for life and capacity to love, in spite of the oppressive existence imposed upon her.

Task 12: Puritan attitudes to women AO3

- The puritanical elements of Gileadean society may strike the reader as anachronistic.
- Although there is evidence of computerised technology in Gilead, Atwood also describes a reaction against certain uses of science and technology particularly in the area of reproductive technologies as there are no abortions, no birth scans and no fertility treatments.
- Atwood depicts a Christian fundamentalist society with literal interpretations of the Bible dictating how lives are lived, and creating a gulf between the function and relative status of men and women in society.

Task 13: Surveillance AO4

- One of the ways in which Gilead is run is through self-surveillance, as people speak and behave guardedly, fearing the consequences of putting a foot wrong.
- The idea of a 'panopticon' could be seen to apply here, a society in which citizens live with the ever-present possibility of being watched. This is represented by the 'eye' tattoo and the 'Eyes' who are the state's secret police.
- In *Nineteen Eighty-Four*, Orwell writes that 'Big Brother is watching you' everywhere in Oceania and describes in considerable detail how this culture of propaganda and surveillance works. Whether Big Brother is a real leader or symbolic figurehead is unclear.
- In stark contrast to Offred, the novel's protagonist Winston Smith works as a clerk at the 'Ministry of Truth', rewriting historical documents and removing 'unpersons'.

PROGRESS CHECK ANSWERS

Part Two: Studying *The Handmaid's Tale*

Section One: Check your understanding

1. Compile a glossary of terms used in Gilead, for example *Ceremony*, *Computalk* and *Econowife*.

- Wife, Commander, Aunt, Handmaid, Econowife, etc. – these names suggest that people's function in society is more important than their individuality in Gilead.

- Martha, Handmaid, Angel, etc. – many names and terms have a scriptural meaning.

- 'Ceremony' – the monthly sexual encounter between Offred, her Commander and his Wife is referred to by a euphemistic proper noun (p. 104). Other events attended by Offred include a Prayvaganza (a mass wedding ceremony) and a Salvaging (public execution).

2. List four or five moments in the novel that show Offred at her most defiant, and comment briefly on the significance of each.

- Offred decides to steal a flower from the sitting room in Chapter 17.

- Nick becomes associated with the illicit and the pleasurable, culminating in Offred's affair with him and the risks she takes to pursue it.

- In Chapter 46, Offred thinks about different ways in which she could escape, e.g. by starting a fire with her match.

- Much of Offred's defiance lies in the way her thoughts, feelings and memories privately pose a challenge to the kind of existence she is supposed to lead.

3. What do we learn about Offred's life and family before Gilead? Make a list.

- We learn about her mother – a single mother and feminist, and she describes a few early memories.

- She was married to Luke, who was divorced, and we learn that it was a happy, loving relationship.

- Offred also recalls her daughter.

- Offred describes her work and her economic independence, and how life started to change as women's freedoms were eroded.

- Her final memories of her family are of their attempts to escape.

4. How is the feminist movement of the 1970s presented in the novel? Write a paragraph summarising your thoughts.

- The second wave feminist movement is embodied in the novel by the figure of Offred's mother.

- The propaganda at the Rachel and Leah Centre portrays this movement as having been problematic and dangerous.

- Atwood's views are nuanced and some ambivalence is suggested, but Offred's narrative overwhelmingly presents the removal of women's freedoms and choices as an unjust abuse of their human rights.

5. Make notes on three violent events that take place in *The Handmaid's Tale*.

- From early on in the novel, Offred describes bodies displayed on the Wall, and as readers we begin to understand the violence and fear on which Gilead is built. There is a reference to a bloody coup in Chapter 28 – and several mentions of ongoing hostilities.

- The Salvagings are the euphemistic term for extra-judicial public hangings. The crimes of the executed women are not revealed.

- The Particicution in Chapter 43 is a particularly violent spectacle in which the Handmaids' vitriol is let loose on a man who turns out to be not (as they are told) a rapist but a dissident.

6. In which chapters do we learn about Ofwarren/Janine? Write a paragraph about her various appearances in the novel.

- Offred and Ofglen encounter a pregnant Ofwarren in Chapter 5. Her manner is proud and triumphant.

- At the Rachel and Leah Centre, a more vulnerable side of Janine is shown when she is testifying. In Gilead, being a victim of sexual assault and giving birth to a baby with abnormalities are considered the fault of the woman.

- She gives birth to a baby girl in Section VIII, although at the Prayvaganza Offred learns that Janine's baby was deemed to be an 'Unbaby' and destroyed.

7. What is the narrative function of the novel's 'Night' sections?

- These are Offred's most private moments, her 'time out'.

- Atwood uses these sections to revisit memories from Offred's recent and more distant pre-Gilead past.

- The 'Night' sections also become associated with forbidden activities of various kinds.

8. What is the significance of Offred's account of the prayers in the sitting room before the Ceremony takes place, as described in Chapters 14 and 15?

- It's a highly descriptive passage within the novel.

- Offred casts not only an observant but also an astutely critical eye over her surroundings.

- In so doing, she challenges the dominant ideology in both its material form and its scriptural foundation with her own **counter-discourse**.

- She also reflects with some irony on the notion of a 'household' and comments that she is like a slave in the 'hold' (91) of a ship.

9. What do we learn about life in Gilead in the accounts of Offred and Ofglen's shopping trips? Make a list.

- The streets seem sterile and empty, and superficially at least pleasant and safe, 'like the beautiful pictures they used to print in the magazines about homes and gardens and interior decoration' (p. 33).

- We learn about various shops including food stores with religious names and the shop 'Soul Scrolls', selling computerised prayers.

- Written signs are being replaced with pictorial ones: 'they decided that even the names of shops were too much temptation for us' (p. 35).

- We also get glimpses of the surveillance, violence and propaganda on which Gilead is built, e.g. the Wall, the Eyes and their black vans, and slogans such as 'GOD IS A NATIONAL RESOURCE' (p. 225) in Chapter 33.

10. List four or five moments in the novel that shed light on the character of the Commander and his role in the novel.

- In Chapter 8, Offred finds him ourside her room 'violating custom' by being there.

- Offred thinks about the strangeness of his role as head of the household before and during the Ceremony.

- Via Nick, the Commander invites Offred to his study and allows her to play Scrabble, read and, later on, to visit Jezebel's.

- Offred asks him some questions including the meaning of the Latin inscription in her room.

- There is an attempt in the 'Historical Notes' to work out his true identity.

11. What is the narrative function of Offred's predecessor – the Commander's previous handmaid 'Offred'? Write a paragraph explaining your ideas.

- Offred feels solidarity with her. They share a 'name', space and function though they are divided by time.
- The words Offred finds in the cupboard interest Offred and give her a mantra she takes strength from repeating.
- She discovers what happened to her predecessor in that room in Chapter 29.

12. Identify where in the novel we learn about the Handmaids' 're-education' for their new role, and make notes about what we learn about this process.

- Handmaids are taught to think differently about their pre-Gilead lives, e.g. 'In the days of anarchy, it was freedom to. Now you are bring given freedom from' (p. 34) and 'We were a society dying … of too much choice' (p. 35).
- The Aunts deliver this re-education to the Handmaids. The Aunts' names are soft and comforting but this is in stark contrast to their message and the violence they can inflict on their students.
- We are offered glimpses of some of the brainwashing activities that take place at the Rachel and Leah Centre, including videos and chanting.

13. What is the signficance of the episodes that take place in the garden? Make a list.

- Like the house itself, the attractive garden reflects the comfortable life led by the Commander and his Wife.
- Although beautiful, there is an emptiness and pointlessness about the time the Commander's Wife spends there, gardening and sometimes knitting scarves: 'Many of the Wives have such gardens, it's something for them to order and maintain and care for' (p. 22).
- It is in the garden that Serena Joy suggests Offred tries to get pregnant by Nick and refers to the possibility of Offred seeing a photograph of her daughter.
- The garden also represents beauty, sensuality and hope for Offred.

14. How does Atwood introduce and develop the idea of an underground resistance movement in Gilead? Write a timeline showing what is revealed and when.

- In Chapter 8, in what could be a coded message, Ofglen says that it's 'a beautiful May day' (p. 53) and on page 177, at Soul Scrolls, Ofglen suggests that Offred 'join us'.
- Moira's story, as retold to Offred at Jezebel's, describes how the 'Underground Railroad' works, how fraught with risk it is, and how brave its members are.
- Nick mentions the 'Mayday' resistance movement in Chapter 46 to reassure Offred.

15. How does Offred write about her body? Write a paragraph discussing your evidence and ideas.

- During the Ceremony in Chapter 16, Offred describes what is happening in 'the lower part of my body' (p. 104), implying a separation between – or an effort to separate – body and brain.
- Offred also describes this kind of separation at the doctor's in Chapter 11: 'He deals with a torso only' (p. 70).
- In other more private moments, Offred writes about her body both as something that has been appropriated by Gilead as a 'resource' and yet which she knows better than anyone – 'a swamp, fenland, where only I know the footing' (p. 83) – suggesting she retains some agency and power in relation to her body.

16. What is the significance to the novel as a whole of Offred's visit to Jezebel's? Make brief notes.

- Offred is allowed to wear revealing clothing but is simultaneously playing out a male fantasy.
- This section of the novel reveals Gilead's hypocrisy in having a state brothel whose workers don't officially exist.
- Offred is able to speak to her friend Moira and learns about what happened to her.

17. List three moments in the novel where Offred questions her own version of events as a narrator. What is the effect of these moments on the reader?

- In Chapter 23, Offred describes why 'it's impossible to say a thing exactly the way it was' (p. 144).
- In Chapter 38, Offred presents what is 'more or less' (p. 255) Moira's story. She tries to use words that sound like Moira as 'way of keeping her alive' (p. 256) but explains that 'we didn't have much time so she just gave the outlines' (p. 255).
- Offred presents visiting Nick in multiple ways in Chapter 40: 'I made that up. It didn't happen that way. Here is what happened' (p. 273) and a little later 'It didn't happen that way either' (p. 275).

18. Write a paragraph outlining what we know about the relationship between Offred and Nick.

- Nick, the Commander's chauffeur, winks at Offred in Chapter 4.
- Later they have a fleeting encounter in the sitting room in Chapter 17. This triggers memories of Luke and contrasts with Offred's sexual encounters with Commander though, ironically, Nick needs to tell Offred that the Commander wants her to come to see him.
- They become increasingly intimate after Chapter 40. She tells him her name, wants to stay where she is to be with him, and believes she is pregnant by him.

19. What do you find striking about the way Atwood presents Offred's exit from the house in Chapter 46?

- Her departure is the culmination of a period of escalating tension in the novel.
- It is also an extremely dramatic event implicating various members of the household and contrasts with the many parts of the novel that are – outwardly at least – uneventful.
- Offred's final comment shows that she is uncertain about her fate at this point: 'And so I step up, into the darkness within; or else the light' (p. 307), and the 'Historical Notes' offer no certainty about Offred's fate.

20. What do the 'Historical Notes' contribute to the novel? Write a paragraph summarising your thoughts.

- Dated June 25, 2195, the 'Historical Notes' take the reader much further into the future. Different voices are speaking, while Offred and the characters we have been reading about are long dead.
- The Republic of Gilead is also shown to be a thing of the past and thus a topic for historians.
- However, Atwood's juxtaposition of the 'Historical Notes' with Offred's long first-person narrative challenges writers of history to consider what their narratives value and what they leave out.

Section Two: Working towards the exam

1. '*The Handmaid's Tale* is a survival narrative'. Discuss.
- Offred is an engaging narrator with whom the reader becomes involved, and we care about her survival – and the survival of her loved ones.
- Atwood writes about the role of the resistance movement in survival – Ofglen and Nick's involvement with Mayday, the links in the Underground Railroad, etc.
- The novel has much to say about the survival of the spirit – and the difficulty of remaining hopeful in such dire circumstances.
- In her descriptions of Gilead, Atwood writes about the means by which values and ideologies survive and how they can be eroded.
- The 'Historical Notes' ask a further set of questions about survival – the physical survival of Offred's 'documents', and the survival within the grand narrative of history of the experiences and perspectives of disempowered, marginal voices.

2. Consider the role of memory in this novel.
- Atwood structures her novel non-chronologically with numerous **flashbacks** and memories from the recent as well as the distant past in the days before Gilead.
- The 'Night' sections are particularly associated with memory, as these are times of reflection and meditation for Offred. However, Offred's memories can resurface in her narrative at other times too, triggered by a word, a place, a scent, etc.
- Offred is determined to remember clearly and also to be honest about the unavoidably fractured and imperfect nature of her memories.
- The novel describes the pain of loss and of not knowing what happened to loved ones. Offred's portraits of Moira, her mother, Luke and her daughter might be read as **elegies** for the missing and the lost.
- Offred describes how unreliable memory is and how even treasured memories begin to fade.

3. What do we learn about the narrator from the way she tells and structures her story?
- Offred is a witty and humorous narrator. She loves – and misses – reading, and enjoys words and wordplay, as shown during the games of Scrabble but also throughout her narrative, e.g. in the description of the garden in Chapter 25.
- We learn of her close relationships with loved ones from her past – and that she misses companionship. We are told she would have liked to develop some kind of friendship with the Commander's Wife, the Marthas, etc.
- First-person narration helps the reader to understand Offred's personal and independent thoughts and feelings and at the same time to appreciate that she must show great self-control and care in her behaviour and speech in Gilead.
- As the novel progresses, Atwood describes more and more secrecy and suspicion, creating both opportunities and threats for Offred.
- Throughout she returns to her memories of the past and to painful speculation about the present and the future, particularly with respect to her loved ones.

4. To what extent is Atwood's novel a love story?
- Many flashbacks in the novel document and reflect Offred's love for her husband and daughter.
- The love between Nick and Offred develops in the closing chapters in the novel against a background of growing danger, suspicion and violence.
- Atwood establishes a powerful contrast between Offred's memories of loving, tender relationships and consensual sex in 'the time before', and her experiences in Gilead where love,

intimacy and sexual pleasure are forbidden and largely absent from people's lives.
- The savagery and brutality of the Gileadean regime reveals an interpretation of Christianity in which love, mercy, forgiveness, etc. do not feature.
- The 'Historical Notes' present Offred's experiences from a post-Gilead perspective, but continue to attach more value to the political events than to the personal ones.

5. Choose three characters from the novel and write about the different ways in which they are shown by Atwood to be victims of the system in Gilead.
- The arc of Janine/Ofwarren's story shows her vulnerability and presents her as a 'victim'. Her moment of pride and triumph in a successful pregnancy is short-lived.
- Another kind of victimhood is seen in Moira's resignation to her fate after fighting against the system so spiritedly for so long.
- The Commander's Wife leads a comfortable life but has been displaced. She spends a great deal of time on what might be seen as futile activities such as knitting, is forced to share her husband, and becomes increasingly suspicious and jealous. Offred reflects that Serena Joy evangelised for a movement that has actually turned her into a victim too.

Part Three: Characters and themes

Section One: Check your understanding

1. What is the significance of Offred's relationship with Nick? Write a paragraph explaining your view.
- Nick is important for his function as Offred's romantic lover.
- Her relationship with Nick becomes more important to Offred than her desire for freedom.
- Nick is possibly a member of the Mayday resistance group; there is a glimmer of hope for Offred when he says, 'It's all right. It's Mayday. Go with them' (p. 305).

2. Make notes on the role of the Aunts in Gilead, and the two contexts in which we see Aunt Lydia – what is our opinion of her character?
- Too old for breeding, the Aunts function as enforcers in Gilead and have the power to deal out punishments.
- The Aunts, and especially Aunt Lydia, are part of the process of 'training' that Offred endures under the state regime.
- We see Aunt Lydia at the Red Centre and at the Salvaging. She is a cruel character, who seems to relish giving out punishments to women under her control.

3. List three ways in which the Republic of Gilead erases Offred's identity as a woman.
- Offred's real name is denied her and is replaced with the patronym 'Of-fred', showing that she is the property of a man.
- Offred must wear the red uniform of a Handmaid, where she is identified only by her gender role.
- In Gilead, women are no longer allowed to write, or read written words. Offred's discovery of the scratched words 'Nolite te bastardes carborundorum' (p. 62) is in itself an act of treachery against the state.

4. Identify three things Offred does which demonstrate her subversive resistance to the regime.
- Offred steals a daffodil from the sitting room.
- Offred uses fragments of remembered story to remind herself who she was before the Republic of Gilead existed.
- In 'a small defiance of rule' (p. 31), Offred makes eye contact with a Guardian.

5. What is the significance of Offred's remembered stories? Write a short paragraph explaining your ideas.

• The theme of imprisonment runs through the novel; Offred's only escape is into her own memory.

• Offred uses memory to keep the absent presences of her husband, daughter, mother and friend with her. Although she is trapped, these memories prevent her from feeling utterly alone.

• In her desperation to believe that her husband has survived, Offred invents different story versions for him, in the hope that he is still alive.

• Offred's stories show the complex way memory works, where thoughts in the present contain traces of previous times.

6. 'The failed dystopia of Gilead can be considered a warning to twentieth century society.' List two issues in contemporary society that come under scrutiny in the novel, and write a short paragraph on each.

• Technology: we think nothing of storing our personal data on computers. Yet the narrative reminds us, 'All they needed to do is push a few buttons' (p. 187). The novel suggests that our easy acceptance of the computer age puts us at risk.

• The environment: Offred says, 'The air got too full, once, of chemicals, rays, radiation, the water swarmed with toxic molecules' (p. 122). In Gilead, many disfigured 'Unbabies' (p. 123) are born, and the primary concern is the fall in the rate of reproduction. The novel can be seen as a critique of our denial of the importance of caring for our environment.

7. Find three instances in the novel where we can see Offred's mother as a heroic figure.

• In pre-Gilead times, Offred's mother was a political activist, campaigning for women's sexual and social freedom.

• Offred's mother resists being dead, returning twice to the narrative, in films that Offred sees while at the Red Centre.

• Offred's mother's political activism shows independence of mind. She defends the idea of being a single parent and Offred comes to admire her courage.

8. Identify three statements or events within Offred's narrative that show how much she is stimulated by her meetings with the Commander in his study.

• Offred enjoys their games of Scrabble; when she handles the letters, she says, 'The feeling is voluptuous. This is freedom' (p. 149).

• After the first evening with the Commander, Offred laughs out loud.

• In the Commander's study, Offred is able to read books: 'I read quickly, voraciously' (p. 194).

9. What is the significance of the men's bodies that hang on the Wall in Chapter 6? Write a paragraph explaining your view.

• They are symbolic of the way that men's identities are stripped away by the Republic of Gilead, too.

• The bodies hang with their heads covered, but Offred begins to restore identity to these men: 'You can see the outlines of the features under the white cloth' (p. 42).

• Blood has seeped through the cloth of one of the men's faces, to form 'another mouth, a small red one' (p. 42). The imagery is a disturbing reminder that this happens to women, too.

10. Make a table listing four or five things we learn from Offred's narrative about Serena Joy's character.

• Offred comments that Serena Joy has nothing to do except knit scarves that are probably 'unravelled and turned back into balls of yarn, to be knitted again' (p. 23).

• Serena Joy has arthritis and walks with a cane.

• Her ageing face is described in detail: 'Two lines led downwards from the corners of her mouth' (p. 25).

• After the copulation ceremony, she lies on her bed like an 'effigy' in an image of death (p. 106).

• Serena Joy's greeting to Offred is cold and unwelcoming: 'You might as well come in' (p. 24).

Section Two: Working towards the exam

1. 'Offred's only freedom in Gilead is that which her imagination provides.' Do you agree?

• Offred escapes the painful reality of her present by using her memories to provide a different narrative to the one which is imposed upon her, and so retains a sense of her identity.

• She uses stories of the loved ones from her past as a way of keeping those absent presences with her.

• At night, when she is alone, she is able to select from her memories to revisit past faces and places: 'the night is my time out. Where should I go?' (p. 47).

• Offred's imagination creates different story versions for her husband, Luke's, fate, so that she can hang on to the belief that he may have survived.

• Her visits to the Commander allow her a different kind of freedom, where she can read books and play Scrabble.

• Offred finds emotional freedom in her loving relationship with Nick.

2. 'Gilead is a state where men hold all the power and women have none.' To what extent do you agree with this statement?

• Women in Gilead can be viewed as having little or no power, as they are labelled with names indicating ownership by men, and they are defined by their gender role.

• A new hierarchy of feminine power has formed within the community of women in Gilead, from the Commanders' Wives to the Marthas, and Offred's role as Handmaid signals her place as breeder in this hierarchy.

• The Aunts wield a brutal power of life or death, as can be seen in the staged Salvagings.

• The Commander is trapped in his role, and his outing with Offred to Jezebel's reveals his yearning for more than the clinical Ceremony where he is observed in copulation each month.

• The Commander's study is a place where the balance of power is altered and where Offred comes to feel she can talk as an equal – but this is underlined by the irony that she is at the Commander's mercy.

• The Republic of Gilead rules through fear and brutality – and Offred lives in constant fear for her life – but men are also victims of state oppression as evidenced in the hangings and the Partiticution ceremony in Chapter 43, where the women exert a terrible power to kill.

3. Compare the characters of Offred, Moira and Ofglen. What models of heroism do they provide?

• Offred's model of resistance is by subversion. She finds 'tiny peepholes' (p. 31) in the regime – small ways in which she can show her defiance.

• Moira is a rebel, who refuses to conform. She makes repeated attempts to escape, and becomes a fantasy of survival for the other, imprisoned women in the Red Centre.

• Ofglen is a resistance fighter who shows a particular kind of courage in the way she acts at the Particicution ceremony. She embodies courage against frightening odds.

• In spite of her irrepressible character, Moira is doomed to the Colonies and in contrast to the colour she brings to Offred's life, she simply fades from the text.

• Ofglen, true to her resistance fighter character, dies a martyr's death by hanging herself.

- Ironically, it is Offred who the novel suggests survives and leaves the reader with a sense of hope – she is motivated not by courage but by her instinct for survival.

Part Four: Genre, structure and language

Section One: Check your understanding

1. List three or four key narrative techniques that Atwood uses which reveal Offred's inner life and sharpness of mind.
- Imagery
- Word play
- Irony; Offred can see the absurdity of her situation in her Scrabble games
- 'Overlay' of past memory with present reality

2. Find three or four examples of images from nature used in the narrative.
- Flowers: 'the tulips are opening their cups' (p. 22)
- Gardens: Serena Joy's garden has 'a lawn in the middle, a willow, weeping catkins' (p. 22)
- Seasons: 'I look out of the dusk and think about its being winter' (p. 304)
- Colour: 'the tulips along the border are redder than ever' (p. 55)
- Light: 'the mist of moonlight before a rain' (p. 304)

3. Make a table listing some of the ways in which Gilead uses biblical language.
- The law enforcers, or 'Guardian Angels', are named after Old Testament figures. The state spies are called 'Eyes of the Lord'.
- Women's roles are given biblical titles, such as Handmaids, and the 'Marthas', from the woman who served Christ.
- The state-run brothel is called 'Jezebel's'.
- The car brand names are 'Behemoth', 'Whirlwind' or 'Chariot'.
- Shops are named from biblical texts: 'Lilies of the Field' and 'All Flesh'.

4. Write a short paragraph explaining how Atwood's narrative uses the female body.
- The narrative contains recurring image of hands, feet, faces, eyes, blood and womb.
- Offred's focus on her own female body reminds her of identity as a woman; it is the source of her emotional survival.
- The language of the body uses poetic imagery to express her emotions and desires.
- In writing about her body, Offred is using a feminine voice which can be heard even when she is muted by the patriarchal order in Gilead.

5. Find two examples where Offred's narrative is outward facing, using 'you'. Explain briefly why she might do this.
- 'Dear You' (p. 49)
- 'I believe you're there' (p. 279)
- Offred invents the reader as a survival technique – she has to believe her voice will be heard by others, to go on living.

6. Make a table listing other Handmaids in the novel. For each, add a note about what happens to them.
- Janine, or Ofwarren: gives birth to an Unbaby. Loses her mind
- Ofglen: hangs herself to avoid torture
- Unnamed woman, who previously inhabited Offred's room: hanged herself
- Two Handmaids at the Salvaging: Ofcharles and a second, unnamed Handmaid. Both hanged

7. Write brief notes explaining Janine's story. List two ways in which she is significant in the novel.
- She first appears at the Red Centre, where she is a willing victim.
- She has a moment of triumph as she gives birth at the Birth Day, but we learn later that the child was an 'Unbaby'.
- She last appears at the Particicution, where she has lost her mind.
- Janine's story follows the career of a Handmaid; she shows the likely outcome for such women in Gilead. She is a warning to Offred of what might happen if she gives up hope.

8. List four or five of the main features of a dystopian society.
- Patriarchal rule
- Totalitarianism and dictatorship
- Strict social hierarchy
- Stripping away of individual difference in the interests of the greater good for all
- State control of language

9. Write a short paragraph explaining why you think an author may write dystopian fiction.
- Dystopian fiction is not just fantasy – it offers a possible model for a future society.
- This kind of writing may make an attack on society; it becomes protest writing.
- Because dystopian fiction may comment on either politics or society, it often aims to teach moral values.
- Works of dystopian fiction may deliver strong warnings against the consequences of particular kinds of political and social behaviour.

10. Write a short paragraph explaining the way the narrative uses flashback.
- The broken nature of the narrative, fragmented as it is by the constant shifts in time achieved by flashback, reflects Offred's shock and disorientation in her new existence.
- Flashback occurs most frequently in the 'Night' sections; these are times when Offred is alone and can explore her memories of the past.
- Offred's flashback sections function as emotional and psychological survival strategies.

Section Two: Working towards the exam

1. 'The Handmaid's Tale is a narrative in which female voices of protest are heard.' To what extent do you agree with this statement?
- Offred's narrative is a voice of protest; she uses imagery which draws on nature and the female body. It is a feminised language which resists the patriarchal regime.
- The unnamed woman who inhabited Offred's room before is silenced by the regime. However we might also think of her words left for Offred: 'Nolite te bastardes carborundorum' (p. 237) as evidence that her voice, however small, is still heard.
- Other voices of women's protest remain unheard, hidden in the stories of Handmaids, such as Ofcharles, who is hanged at the Salvaging.
- Women's voices are muted by the regime's control of language: Moira's attempt to sing a rebellious version of 'There is a Balm in Gilead' (p. 230) is muffled by the Handmaids' choir, while Offred can only pray in private.
- Offred attempts to project her voice into the far future, but the professor's speech in the 'Historical Notes' reduces and undermines her so that, finally, her protest remains unheard.

2. Consider ways in which *The Handmaid's Tale* might be considered as political and social protest writing.

- The main concerns of political and social protest writing are oppression, power and powerlessness. Such writing seeks to comment on, or criticise, aspects of society. It often depicts rebellion in a corrupt society.

- Offred operates from a position of powerlessness and she resorts to subversion. Her poetic narrative voice and rich overlay of remembered stories resists Gilead's attempt to flatten and homogenise and in this way, Offred offers us a model of rebellion.

- Ofglen's model of rebellion is as a resistance fighter, while Moira's model is rebellion through her refusal to conform or submit.

- The Commander symbolises corrupt society – he upholds the rules of Gilead at the same time as he breaks them by secretly meeting with Offred and taking her to the brothel.

- Political and social protest writing may also examine the ways that society uses language; many biblical references have been perverted by Gilead in order to control.

3. 'I'm sorry there is so much pain in this story. I'm sorry it's in fragments, like a body caught in crossfire' (p. 279). Discuss the ways in which Atwood has chosen to present Offred's story to us.

- Offred's story weaves accounts of everyday life with fragments of remembered story chiefly told in the 'Night' sections. In her 'external' sections where she pictures for us her present, bleak existence, Offred's voice is distanced and lacking in emotion: 'One detaches oneself. One describes' (p. 106).

- In contrast, in the 'Night' sections, her language is vivid and rich with imagery which reveals her own enthusiasm for life, in spite of the oppressive regime she lives under. It is here we gain a sense of her feminine language of nature and the body.

- The way the stories of past and present are woven together means that the narrative is presented as fragmented, or broken; we share Offred's shock and dread at the likely outcomes for her family members as we gradually piece together a picture of what happened before Gilead.

- Offred says, 'We lived in the gaps between the stories' (p. 67). We gain a sense of her real pain and anguish from the blanks between the text where she is unable to describe.

- Offred's story is reconstructed in a future where Gilead no longer exists; Atwood presents Offred's words as enduring beyond her perilous present and in this way the story becomes a narrative of survival.

Part Five: Contexts and interpretations

Section One: Check your understanding

1. In what ways does *The Handmaid's Tale* reflect political and religious developments in the USA in the 1980s? Make brief notes.

- In her novel, Atwood reflects on the increasing popularity of the views and values of the American New Right in the United States throughout the 1980s.

- Atwood's description of Gilead's punishment by death for gay people and for doctors who perform abortions can be seen as a comment on views she perceived to be gaining in popularity at the time.

- Her characterisation of the Commander's Wife – previously known as a religious singer on television – may be based on one or more prominent women within this movement, and reflects the growth in televangelism during the late 1970s and

the 1980s.

2. Write a paragraph about *The Handmaid's Tale* in the context of the science fiction genre and/or other dystopian novels.

- Atwood's novel is set in the near future, and this connection to the present is a feature of dystopian writing, which serves to some degree as a warning of things to come. George Orwell's *Nineteen Eighty-Four* and P. D. James's *The Children of Men* were also set in the relatively near future at the time of writing.

- The nameless narrator of Doris Lessing's *The Memoirs of a Survivor* and Offred could be compared as female protagonists and first-person narrators.

- Thematically, comparisons could be drawn between Atwood's novel and a number of futuristic novels including J. G. Ballard's *The Drowned World* (environmental issues), *The Children of Men* (a global fertility crisis) and *Brave New World* (attitudes to sex and reproduction).

- The techniques that Atwood uses to render her locations and picture of the future believable include using real places and using a first-person narrator to give the impression of a real eyewitness testimony. These techniques are also used in *The War of the Worlds* and *Frankenstein*.

3. What should we infer from Offred's description of the Commander's house and garden about the Commander and the Commander's Wife? List three key points.

- The Victorian house is comfortable, and details about its appearance and furnishings suggest its owners are successful and respectable people.

- Yet Atwood also conveys the idea that while they may superficially seem comfortable, the deeper truths about the household and the ideology that underpins it breed unhappiness, suspicion and discomfort.

- There is a contrast between the stale and suffocating atmosphere of the house and the garden, in which Offred finds beauty and hope.

4. Make a table listing at least three points of connection between *The Handmaid's Tale* and another literary text you have studied. (example: William Blake's *Songs of Innocence and Experience*)

- Blake's collection of poems and Atwood's novel are written in very different eras but are both concerned with political and social conditions and their consequences.

- They both express the view that humans have the potential to flourish but can become like prisoners.

- Blake opposes 'innocence' with 'experience'; Atwood contrasts the present day with a dystopian future vision.

- Religious allusions are used in both texts in differing ways.

5. List three to four events or situations that might provide focal points for a feminist reading of this novel.

- Atwood writing about her body in Chapter 13 and elsewhere

- Offred's mother in the time before and different presentations of, and attitudes to, feminism that are explored in the novel

- The nature of the re-education that Handmaids receive at the Rachel and Leah Centre

- Moira and her escape attempts

- The 'romance' narrative between Offred and Nick

6. How is the dominant ideology in Gilead enforced? List three or four ways and include specific references to the text.

- Importance of attendance at mass public events

- Brainwashing, serious threats (such as fear of death or being sent to the Colonies) and other forms of violence

- With the passing of time, the status quo would begin to seem more natural as people would not know anything different

- Lack of access to books, public transport, etc. and use of propaganda in media channels and education

7. To what extent would you describe *The Handmaid's Tale* as a 'multi-voiced narrative'? Write a paragraph explaining your viewpoint.

- Offred's voice is a complex one, adopting different tones and styles.
- Offred often doubts her abilities as a storyteller and sometimes gives more than one version of events.
- She retells Moira's story as if Moira were telling it, as a tribute to her friend.
- The 'Historical Notes' very explicitly bring in other voices to the narrative with a completely different perspective on events.

8. What kind of insights might be gained from a New Historicist reading of *The Handmaid's Tale*? Make brief notes.

- An assortment of non-literary texts that informed Atwood's perspective about key political, social and environmental issues can be read in conjunction with Atwood's novel to support the reader's understanding of North American politics, society and culture in the 1980s.
- The 'Historical Notes' overtly deal with the process by which historical narratives come into being, and are read and valued. Atwood shows us how Offred's narrative has survived as a document, but its treatment and evaluation by the Cambridge historian Pieixoto is often dismissive.
- The reader might also reflect on Gilead's undermining of literacy among its citizens through lack of access to the written word. Even the Bible, whose language permeates so much of public life in Gilead, is kept under lock and key and read only by a privileged few. Offred describes it as an 'incendiary device' (p. 98).

9. Write a paragraph explaining how a critical work you have read has enhanced your understanding of the relationship between language and power within this novel.

- An example of New Historicist criticism, e.g. how history reconstructs the past, whose voices are heard, looking at the 'Historical Notes' in relation to the novel as a whole
- An example of Foucauldian criticism, e.g. how power relationships in Gilead are expressed through language
- An example of feminist criticism, e.g. looking at the role of language and texts in support of a hierarchical patriarchal society in Gilead

10. Refer to three extracts from the novel in which Offred writes about the human body, and make references to relevant critical perspectives.

- Offred's description of her lack of control over what is done to her body when visiting the doctor, during the Ceremony, etc. shows how her body is appropriated and exploited by Gilead – feminist and psychoanalytical criticism
- Offred's description of her body in Chapter 13 uses powerful poetic imagery to convey complex feelings about her bodily sensations, cycles and potential – Cixous's theory of *écriture feminine*
- The function of the bodies hanging from the Wall and what they signify to the Gileadean people in terms of upholding the dominant ideology – Foucault's ideas about discipline, punishment and power

Section Two: Working towards the exam

1. Consider the significance of surveillance in *The Handmaid's Tale* and in any other dystopian novel you have studied.

- Atwood's frequent use of the motif of 'eyes' creates a sense of a culture in which everyone is watched and no one has a private life.
- This can be compared with the telescreens in George Orwell's *Nineteen Eighty-Four* that survey the population for evidence of thoughtcrime and facecrime, and also with Yevgeny Zamyatin's panopticon-like One State in *We*.
- Orwell also describes the use of spies. In *Nineteen Eighty-Four*, brainwashing starts young and there are many reports of children who have betrayed their parents to the Thought Police. This is linked to the 'doubling' of the Handmaids on shopping trips – Offred wonders if Ofglen might be a spy and Janine is suspected by the Aunts.
- The extent to which Offred's body is seen to belong to Gilead and her lack of control over her body and its reproductive potential is another highly invasive form of surveillance being used in Atwood's novel.
- The use of reproductive technologies to take power away from people and place it in the hands of the state is also a key feature of the society that Aldous Huxley describes in *Brave New World*.

2. 'There is no power without resistance.' What different kinds of resistance feature in Atwood's novel?

- Offred resists Gileadean ideology privately in her wide-ranging thoughts and feelings, and these moments are captured in her first-person narrative.
- Small actions like a kiss or a theft can also be a form of resistance.
- As Offred says at the Wall in Chapter 6, she finds it essential to 'be very clear, in my own mind' (p. 43), to retain a perspective that is capable of making distinctions and thinking critically.
- Offred also uses humour to, in her own mind at least, satirise and belittle powerful people and institutions.
- Atwood also describes more organised forms of resistance including the 'Mayday' group and Moira's struggle against the system.

3. How does Atwood make use of debates about the methods and objectives of the second wave feminist movement in her novel?

- In Chapter 7, Offred describes a memory of attending a feminist magazine-burning with her mother and presents Offred's mixed feelings about the magazines as a young girl as compared with the staunchly negative views held by her mother and her friends.
- Atwood is perhaps protesting here against dogma, against holding inflexible positions on issues that are very complex. She also suggests that different generations of women may hold different views and have different priorities.
- The Aunts' position is presented as an assault on women's rights and freedoms as we know them. The Aunts characterise the feminist movement as responsible for the problems in society that needed to be addressed and refer to such women as 'Godless' 'Unwomen'. (p. 129)
- The undoing of the successes of the feminist movement (the freedoms that Offred perhaps took for granted) is ultimately what Atwood shows to be at the root of Offred's suffering in the novel. She has no rights over her child, her body, her movement, her reproduction, her sexual partners – all have been taken away.

MARK SCHEME

Use this page to assess your answer to the **Practice task** provided on page 98.

Look at the elements listed for each Assessment Objective. Examiners will be looking to award the highest grades to the students who meet the majority of these criteria. If you can meet two to three elements from each AO, you are working at a good level, with some room for improvement to a higher level.*

> As an example of political and social protest writing, a major concern of *The Handmaid's Tale* is the rebellion of the individual against systems of power. To what extent do you agree with this view in relation to the novel?

AO		
AO1	Articulate informed, personal and creative responses to literary texts, using associated concepts and terminology, and coherent, accurate written expression.	• You make a range of clear, relevant points about rebellion by a range of characters within the novel, eg. Ofglen and Moira. • You use a range of literary terms correctly, e.g. narrative voice, flashback, irony, metaphor, alliteration. • You address the topic clearly across the text, outlining your thesis and providing a clear conclusion. • You signpost and link your ideas fluently about rebellion and systems of power within *The Handmaid's Tale*. • You offer a personal interpretation which is insightful, well-argued and convincing.
AO2	Analyse ways in which meanings are shaped in literary texts.	• You explain the techniques and methods Atwood uses to present the way that individuals rebel, e.g. through Offred's narrative voice and the way the narrative is structured to recover her identity. • You explain in detail how such examples shape meaning in the text, e.g. you explain how the palimpsestic text overlays Offred's bleak present with vibrant, sensory detail from her past. • You comment on spoken language, setting and structure in a thoughtful, sustained way.
AO3	Demonstrate understanding of the significance and influence of the contexts in which literary texts are written and received.	• You demonstrate your understanding of political and social protest writing tropes, presentations of victims and perpetrators, notions of guilt and innocence, agency, punishment and atonement. • Literary context: Offred's resistance is a feminine reworking of masculine dystopias such as George Orwell's *Nineteen-Eighty Four*, which also focuses on the individual's capacity to resist totalitarian state rule. • Historical or social contexts: Gileadean systems of power are underpinned by ideas drawn from the right-wing, anti-feminist movement in America in the early 1980s, which was strongly religious.
AO4	Explore connections across literary texts.	• You make relevant links between characters and ideas within a text, noting for example how Moira resists by reappearing and Offred's mother is written back into the text in film and anecdote. • You make critical judgements about the approach to resistance or rebellion in *The Handmaid's Tale*, drawing comparisons and contrasts, for example commenting on Atwood's use of a feminised language in Offred's narrative voice and how this manipulates the masculine dystopian form.
AO5	Explore literary texts informed by different interpretations.	• Where appropriate, you incorporate and comment on critics' views of the extent to which the novel can be seen as in terms of resistance or rebellion against systems of power. • You assert your own independent view clearly.

* This mark scheme gives you a broad indication of attainment, but check the specific mark scheme for your paper/task to ensure you know what to focus on.